Leap WRITE In!

Adventures in Creative Writing to S-T-R-E-T-C-H & Surprise Your One-of-a-Kind Mind

Karen Benke

ROOST BOOKS

Boston & London • 2013

Roost Books
An imprint of Shambhala Publications, Inc.
Horticultural Hall
300 Massachusetts Avenue
Boston, Massachusetts 02115
roostbooks.com

Page 278 constitutes a continuation of the copyright page.

9 8 7 6 5 4 3 2

Printed in the United States of America

⊗ This edition is printed on acid-free paper that meets the
American National Standards Institute z39.48 Standard.
♻ Shambhala makes every effort to print on recycled paper.
For more information please visit www.shambhala.com.

Distributed in the United States by Penguin Random House LLC
and in Canada by Random House of Canada Ltd

Designed by Lora Zorian

LIBRARY OF CONGRESS CATALOGING-IN-PUBLICATION DATA

Benke, Karen.
Leap write in!: adventures in creative writing to s-t-r-e-t-c-h
& surprise your one-of-a-kind mind / Karen Benke.—1st ed.
p.   cm.
Includes index.
ISBN 978-1-61180-015-9 (pbk.: alk. paper)
1. English language—Composition and exercises—Juvenile literature.
2. Fiction—Authorship—Juvenile literature. 3. Creative writing—Juvenile literature.
[1. English language—Composition and exercises. 2. Creative writing.]
I. Title.
LB1576.B439 2013
808'.042071—dc23
2012037075

for Nina & Joan who love & listen

for Collin, Luc, Dane, Evan & Nicholas—and for you
who risk finding your own voice . . .

It takes courage to grow up and turn out to be who you really are.

—e.e. cummings

CONTENTS

NEW ARRIVALS, THIS WAY . . .

This book is a passport to gain entry into the wild territory of your expanding heart and widening imagination. No visas, vaccinations, or luggage required. Stamped on these pages are maps and shortcuts to guide you through the portals of your life, into the tangled jungle of Y-O-U. This book's an inward-bound adventure, a way to shake things up from the inside, break you out of any goal-oriented, good-grade focus—or too-cool-for-school defiance—and unleash what you most need and want to say.

Growing up, you see, hear, taste, smell, and feel a lot. Fear, excitement, anxiety, joy, boredom, disappointment, jealousy, desire, confusion, and expectation are all emotions you're probably familiar with by now—even if you don't always want to admit it. Having felt your feelings, though, they become *more* yours and are some of the best tools you have for deepening your creativity and finding your writing voice. Everything about you—strange thoughts, intense feelings, distant memories, vivid dreams, quick observations, slow heartbreaks, life-changing events, and endless surprises—are yours to give to your writing. Toss in edginess, a hint of attitude, a dash of sass. Mix shyness with kindness. Pour in courage. Shake in wonder. Stir up these feeling-ingredients and your writing will shine with more of the real y-o-u, so your readers and fellow travelers can glimpse that glow of *you-ness* that lives on the inside.

There's no way around it: expressing your life on the page is going to require you to take some r-i-s-k-s. This might include leaping over piled-up excuses that start with "But . . ." But I don't have the right kind of talent, notebook, place to sit . . . But my hair's a mess . . . But I need a snack . . . But who cares what I think? . . . But if it's not required, why should I? (I still leap—and occasionally trip—over all the same excuses.) As your guide-on-the-side, I'm going to suggest you begin with a calming breath to relax and reset any and all expectations. Remember: you're in charge of your life (when you're writing and when you're not). You decide how far into your heart you venture, how high into your imagination you fly, or how on-the-surface of gravity you stay.

All the wacky, confusing, brave, soul-stirring wonderings and wanderings of your life begin right here, right now, right where you are. With a pen and this book, you're set for the trip. I'll give you on-the-spot drops, questions to surprise yourself, story starters, mini memoirs, and untie-your-mind lists, which are all intended to inspire you to create one-of-a-kind poems, stories, imaginative fragments, and real-life sketches to share, or not. No deadlines. No grades. Escort your inner critic the "h–e–double hockey sticks" outta here. This book is meant to shake up your one-of-a-kind mind, heart, memory bank, and changing emotional landscape. Take the risks that fit—then, *leap!*

Your friend,

Karen

S-T-R-E-T-C-H

Stretch out with your feelings.

—Obi-Wan Kenobi

Wherever you are, find a place to s-p-r-a-w-l and slow your life *waaaay* down for a spell. Drape over your desk, a chair, your bed. Hang like a rag doll in a forward bend. Rise to stand with your feet rooted square on the ground. Lift an arm up and over, leaning to the side like a crescent moon (waxing or waning, you decide). Feel the yawn of your ribs. Fill up each squishy pink lung. Kick off your shoes. Say hello to knees, chins, ankles, and painted or unpainted toenails. Raise your spine—and writing life—skyward. With eyes closed listen to the wavelike sounds of your breath's gentle crash and retreat. You can't do this sprawly-stretchy-bendy-breathy stuff wrong. Just hang out awhile and observe the unique way that oxygen swirls in and out of your body.

Once you're relaxed and used to creating that ocean wave sound of your breath, consider what else stretches. A wishful thought, a white lie, the idea of time, a parent's indecision, your curfew. How far can your mind stretch into the truth of right now? And the next right now, and the next? Whatever the truth is to you, with its noisy demands, itchy worries, or rash-like anxieties, write it. Exactly as is. Don't change a thing. Not that fed-up sigh or give-me-a-break roll of your eyes. Invite it *all* to crawl out into a long s-t-r-e-t-c-h across the length of your page.

Drop Deeper

- Finish the following starters. Forget about punctuation, correct spelling, the finish line. Stretch sense into nonsense, nonsense back into sense. Bring whatever you're feeling along for the ride. When you think you're through, unfurl twenty more word-clues about you.

Life keeps giving me

- verbal sword fights and broken bits of heart-logic; hieroglyphic
- dreams and a sea-green passport to spiraled feelings; a muddy
- bank at low tide, and the bend in my left knee where an over-
- stretched ligament snapped, and life as I knew it changed this
- fast.

Life isn't giving me _____.

Here's why I leave _____.

Here's why I stay _____.

Here's what lights me up _____.

Here's what darkens my heart _____.

Life isn't giving me bridges or snowcapped peaks. Not today.
Life isn't giving me my choice to say *please* or *thank you*.
Here's why I stay: I'm afraid to go.
Here's what lights me up: fresh air, cool friends,
making footprints across the wet earth.
Here's what darkens my heart: a mismatched pair of socks,
one red, one white, a deepening trail of twilight,
a heartbreaking story that unties all the knots.

—Group poem by Ryan, Kalia, Lola

Your Turn

WHAT MATTERS?

Follow your inner moonlight; don't hide the madness.

—Allen Ginsberg

Give yourself a slope of grass and time to daydream, to write what matters most to you. Right now. A list, with details. Not just my friends, but Lynn asking, "Hey, Kare-Bear. Wanna go for a scoop of ge-la-to?" Or the way Collin slides a ping-pong paddle into my hand, challenging: "Best out of three!" As you write, don't hide your madness. Let it be OK to doodle that dream scene where you're walking to school in your underwear, and your bff turns to you and says, "Girlfriend, this ain't no dream. What *are* you doing?"

Ask yourself what small objects matter. That snow globe souvenir with the Eiffel Tower, the bucket of heart-shaped stones on the porch, those ticket stubs saved from museums, movies, concerts. What other things matter to you? A red straw hat, tufts of cotton candy, and a ride on the Tilt-A-Whirl once mattered to me. The partings of atoms and air as a baseball slices center field to fall into your mitt might matter to you. Your determination, a new house, a song lyric, a playful nudge from your new crush.

You choose. Or don't choose, and include them all. Give your examples extra *oomph* by borrowing original details from your original life. (Name names, pets, addresses.) Expose what catches your attention and holds heat. I read somewhere that specificity is generosity. So be specific—and generous—as you gather up what matters, to ignite your word-fire. Places to look for what matters: between, around, inside, underneath everywhere that you can completely be yourself, without the need to please or prove anything to anybody.

Drop Deeper

- What word, sandwich, coin, city, question, sport, number, letter, ice cream flavor, snatch of dialogue, and memory matter to you? What matters today can and will change tomorrow.
- Arrange a random series of questions, imagining what common items found around your town or in nature might matter to other nearby things. Go for twenty lines (or more), the way Judyth did.

What Matters

What matters? Who matters? Does it matter? What is matter?
Does the wind matter to the trees?
Does a crumb matter to an ant?
Does the tire matter to the truck?
Does love matter to me?

Time space matter is one continuum . . .
What matter matter matters most?
What matter matter matters least?
Does a penny matter to the bank?

Does lint matter to the light?
Does red matter to a rose?
Does love matter to me?

What's a matter? Who's a matter?
Is there anything the matter?
Matter splattered all over my face.
Matter hattered all over my head.
Matter tattered all over my bones.
Matter shattered all over my heart.
Does it matter?

—Judyth Collin

Your Turn

_____

_____

_____

_____

_____

_____

_____

_____

_____

_____

_____

_____

_____

_____

_____

_____

_____

_____

_____

Suddenly a Story......

PRACTICING FAREWELL

The dog sits at the top of the stairs. Don't go, the look in his brown eyes begs. Don't leave me alone with an empty bowl where my kibble's meant to be. It's hard, this leaving. How to convince him it's only for a school day? You'll return from basketball practice, walk him to the park, let him roll in the dirt, toss his tennis ball through the dark. You'll sneak him a bite of your burger and chunk of corn bread, whistle him up to your bed, where he turns three circles, curls near your pillow, and slaps a steady beat with his tail. Perhaps his gaze is part of your training. He's testing you as you leave the house, yet again, step onto the welcome mat, and double-lock the door between you. Today's lesson, he says in his silent way, peeking out from under the window curtain, is to trust yourself. The same way you trust he won't chew up your jersey or your mom's new couch cushion. *Be good,* you mouth. *I will,* he barks. Just as you will continue to study long and hard what matters most: to trust your heart's adventure before taking your final exam.

Story Starters

- What look does your dog, cat, hamster, snake give you? Translate a few whines, barks, howls, meows, scurries, and slithers from *their* point of view. Use this for a story opening.

- Who's your wisest four-legged teacher? Who's your most fun two-legged friend?
- Write a story about how you and a favorite pet met . . . or how you said farewell.

Your Turn

_____

_____

_____

_____

_____

_____

_____

_____

_____

_____

_____

_____

Definition Decoder

MEMOIR

Memoirs are like autobiographies, but they tend to only cover a slice of the author's life, not his or her entire birth to near-to-death existence. A writer named Gore Vidal said, "A memoir is how one remembers one's own life."

If you choose to write a memoir, you have to make choices about what particular point(s) in your life you plan to explore. Just your childhood? Everything that happened in sixth grade? The year your parents got divorced? The summer you and your cousin hiked through northern Greece? Or possibly that endless day you had all your braces removed and glued back on? Memoir writers begin by making a list to help them remember specific life turning points. A glittery decision. A jet-propelled regret. A four-layered choice they embraced or wish they could erase. Before you begin, flip through a photo album and select a few moments *behind* your favorite images. Maybe you'll write about a key person who made a huge impact on you (a coach, teacher, dog, sibling), or a series of goals you set and worked hard to achieve. The first play you wrote and directed, making the varsity tennis team as a freshman, sailing around the Mediterranean with your grandparents. Feel the wind at your back as your list gains momentum and your creativity gathers inspiration.

Throughout this book, you'll find mini-memoir examples from my life and suggested experiments to encourage you to explore your life, so that you can locate the slice of story you most want and need to tell. Below are the very beginnings of two young writers' memoirs.

Me and My Sister

What a wonderful thing: I'm seven, my sister, eleven. We laugh riding our bikes past 7-Eleven. Her breath's the exact flavor of cinnamon as she sings that mocking song that's so annoying: *I know you are, but what am I? I know you are, but what am I?* Her eyes are like big blue time machines. Her lips, cracked like crusty bread.

—Grace

Chessy in the Future

I wonder what my life will be like. Will I surf up the road? Will I still have braids that whip around my face? Will I feel free with my spirit like I do now, floating light and gentle like a summer breeze? Will I still rollerblade and think of my black lab, Pari? Will my heart continue to be a rose burning from so much love?

—Chessy

THE GILLUM SHORTCUT

We ride the number 7 bus home from school every day in second grade. Me, Kristin, Paisley, Betsy. The yellow doors swing wide and we all jump off on Fairway Drive in front of the vacant lot we call the Gillum Shortcut, on account of Betsy Gillum's fort-like house at the bottom. We make our way down a steep hill, through a grove of willow trees, to get to the road we live on. Across tall grass, broken glass, dirt mounds, and prickly weeds, we trudge wearing our backpacks. The only thing that can stop us is Betsy's older brother, Mike.

Mike beats us home from school, since he knows a different shortcut. He's the one who hangs Betsy's dolls from ropes tied to the branches of the willow trees. Mike wears camouflage pants and black fatigues and tries to recruit us into his army. He tells us it doesn't matter that we're girls. He says it like that, in two syllables—*gi-rls*. He says he can still teach us to shoot and follow orders. Mike's eyes remind me of the rats we keep in the science room at school. He squints and gets this faraway look when we chant, "No way, Mike!" That's when we know to make a run for it. Fast. All the way to the bottom. No stopping. No one dares look back. Our shortcut is booby-trapped with danger and pockmarked with adventure, one I wouldn't dream of *not* taking to get home.

With Kristin in the lead and her sister, Paisley, shrieking behind me, we laugh and scream, terrified Mike's really going to get us this time. My heart pounds in my ears as I imagine flinging my front door wide and bounding inside to find my mom in the kitchen. I have a life that allows me to be brave, that gives me courage to take risks and detours, my kneesocks ringed with dirt and dotted with prickly burrs. I yell a sharp good-bye over my shoulder to Kristin, promise to meet up after homework, then take a last glance back, across the street, knowing wherever Betsy is, she must be with Mike. Yikes.

Slice of Your Life

- Detail the route up, down, in, through a shortcut you've taken.
- What scary something happened to you or someone you know? What words and images still thrum through you? Write in present tense, as if it's happening right now, like I do.
- What do you carry in your pocket, backpack, head, heart?
- Where do you roam without adults?

Your Turn

PLACES TO BE

I've been things and seen places.
—Mae West

Pick a place—ordinary, made-up, scary, secret, steep, creepy—and lickety-split dash out details of what you'd find there. (I picked the marsh near my house where there's mud, frogs, logs, thorny weeds, egrets, wispy clouds, cattails, mosquitoes, and a slippery bank to sit on and daydream.) Then write down five feelings or states of being you know well (like loneliness, hunger, anger, excitement, fear). Match one feeling to one place and, via metaphor, turn each feeling *into* each place. Easy. (You'll be making an extended metaphor.) For example: Loneliness is a marsh of cattails where egrets swoop through wispy clouds and I wish the frogs in muddy meditation would share their throaty wisdom.

Maybe your anger turns into the Tropics with its scorching beaches and sunburned tourists. Maybe hunger is a closed café on the corner of Thirty-Thirst and Exhaustion where you count your blisters and dream of being home with your sister eating macaroni and cheese, drinking lemonade. You get the picture.

Marsh	Lagoon	Playground
Meadow	Tree house	Dungeon
Rooftop	Café	Grocery store
Basement	Fire station	Laundromat
Heaven	Fort	Castle
River	Space station	Swamp
Tepee	Stadium	Library
Lighthouse	Attic	Carnival
Campground	Basketball court	Concert
Baseball field	Kitchen	Desert
Castle	Classroom	Hell
Deserted island	Palace	Surprise party
Garden	Alley	Rainforest
Big city	Bedroom	Football field
Small town	Garage	Sewer
Forest	Beach	Sailboat
Mountaintop	Tennis court	Milky Way galaxy

SEVEN-LINE CHAIN OF TIME

Write what's in front of your nose.
—William Carlos Williams

D rop your backpack. Gaze out the nearest window. Breathe—through your nose—to a slow count of three, exhaling the same route out. Puff out your lungs as you move your attention to areas in your body where oxygen might never have touched, and galaxies of unexplored space await.

If you can make your exhalation a little longer, this might center a jumpy mind. (It does mine.) Besides carrying oxygen to the brain, the breath is like a key that can unlock the creative magic inside of us, bring our mind and body back together, and help us become victorious over our thoughts. Plus poems and stories will unfold *a lot* easier when you're calm and centered. It's this simple: direct the kind of attention to your breath that you'd give a close friend you haven't seen all summer, then just watch. The way you breathe gives clues about what you're feeling. And since the most important feeling you'll ever have is the feeling you have about yourself, this could come in handy when you write into those undiscovered regions of y-o-u.

Pick seven words. Any seven. Noun words, verb words, weather words, color words, state-of-being words: scared, hungry, bored, sleepy, weepy, joyful words. Words that leap from your imagination, dash out of your heart, bungee jump off the page. Look around, listen, sniff out a few. There are trillions to choose from. And you only need a lucky seven. Write your seven down the center of the page, leaving "breathing room" between each one. Then connect your seven into a chain—necklace, bracelet, or anklet—of time, stringing together other words to jangle along the same stanza (rhyming words, sighing words, laughing, thinking, wordy words, even those woe-is-me-I-forgot-to-breathe words).

Drop Deeper

- I chose: risk, blue, eager, nest, gateway, water, adventure. Use my words to see where your word-connecting leads or choose your own. Bushwhack a word-trail and let it take you where you need to go.

Why only foxes on that **cloudy** day?
Find one **bird**, unique in its own way,
not **afraid** to be different.
Shout out
to the bare **black** trees—
"We're not all the same!" Stand on **grass**
wet with dew. Hope. **Glimpse** a change.

—Elizabeth

This is the **beginning**.
The world of peaked **questions** is in front of you.
You are entering the first chapter of your **life** story.
At the end of this **story**
is the first full **day** of your life.
But first, a **quick** question—
Are you **ready?**

—Jack

Your Turn

Surprise Yourself Survey

SHAPE-SHIFTER ADVENTURE

I have been circling for thousands of years, and I still don't
know if I am a falcon, a storm, or a great song.
—*Rainer Maria Rilke*

My first shape-shifter adventure was with a modern-day
shaman named Susie who guided me into a wild series
of late-night shape-shifts where the images I imagined I became! I
was sitting at my desk by the window in my blue office, safe in my
swirly cloud pajamas, with cat Clive purring by my side. Shaman
Susie, sitting somewhere north of where I live, had a voice clear as
a temple bell over the phone line. With my permission, she led me
to imagine myself in the form of a comet, a mole, a thunderclap, a
rabbit—with spectacles, of course—and then as a great white bird
who soared over the treetops of my neighborhood, flight feathers
filled with moonlight and freedom, leaving behind all the doubt I'd
been bound up by an instant before.

If you want to shape-shift, I know how to guide you across
the page. The only requirement is that you *trust* the dreaming
side of your mind and *let go* of all fear. The imagination is sensitive and can hide itself in a flash if judged, criticized, treated

harshly, or feared. Take this radical challenge: be brave *and* kind to yourself at the same time, when you're writing and even when you're not.

When ready, draw a line down the center of your paper, and use the left side to answer questions 1–8. No need to make 2 + 2 = 4 sense. 2 + 2 = 5 sense is useful when changing your shape.

1. Turn yourself into something that flies or slithers:

a noble raven, a black mamba, a hippogriff, a shooting star, a sneaky sloth, a shy salamander, a baby rattlesnake, a swarm of ladybirds, butterflies, or killer bees.

2. Turn yourself into a kind of weather or natural disaster.

_____

3. Turn yourself into something that runs or leaps.

_____

4. Turn yourself into a shade or color. (Before it, toss in a modifying word, such as *bendy, wet, splashy, tangled*).

_____

5. Turn yourself into a sound—one you hear, or one your ears *can't* hear.

_____

6. Turn yourself into *a dark cave* or *a new hiding place*.

_____

7. Turn yourself into *a midnight flight* or *a meandering dream.*

_____

8. Turn yourself into a specific location in nature. (Describe it.)

_____

Staying with your shape-shifter life, on the right side of your page choose and write down one option from each of the eight choices that follow. If you can't choose, use whatever words please you. It's OK to mix, match, and recombine your answers.

1. *Recent history* or *ancient history,* or the *past,* the *present,* or the *future.*

_____

2. *Swirling inspiration* or *zigzaggy imagination.* Supply your own modifier, if you prefer.

_____

3. *A new beginning* or *a new ending.*

_____

4. *Shadows* or *fog, destiny* or *despair.*

_____

5. *Lost time* or *found time, hunger* or *thirst.*

_____

6. Pick a number between 1 and 100, then pick a word like *journeys, doorways, time zones, poems.*

_____

7. *Dark joy* and/or *bright sadness.*

_____

8. Wild card: pick a favorite word or string of words to write before or after the word *light* (*roaming light, gathered light*).

_____

Write one of the following words between each column: *of, with, into, and, through* (or a word you like better). Draw arrows to attach your answers from the left and right columns. Use the leaping-off lines in the next chapter to continue your shape-shifting adventure.

SHAPE-SHIFTER LEAP-OFF LINES

Be careless, reckless! Be a lion! Be a pirate! when you write.
—Brenda Ueland

There are times you want to write about your experience from the first-person "I" point of view. Other times it's sweet relief to let go of your identity, forget the mighty "I," and observe life from a distance. If you'd like to live within a *different* pronoun during your shape-shift journey, substitute "She," "He," or "We" for "I." Like in a dream, we all have the imaginative powers to change into something new.

A seventh grader named Niko did this. He trudged into first-period English and within minutes of untying his mind to shape-shift, emerged into a swirling gray fog, then ran, gaining speed, through the confusing cave of his imagination where he soared within a hurricane over thirty-one clocks, his spirit tumbling back into his body where he transformed himself and burst forth into a smile of dark joy. (I smiled back.)

I become

I call forth

I cross over

I turn into

I dive into

I'm returned to

I leave behind

I circle back

I'm changed by

I open into

I pass through

I burst forth

I crawl

I swoop

I leap

I soar through

I change into

I glide

I travel between

I weave through

I morph

I tunnel into

I hover above

I reach for

I step into

I twist into

I remember that

I emerge

I inspire myself to

I'm transported by

I wriggle through

I brush past

I'm submerged into

I transmute into

I swerve between

I bend through

I stretch into

I plunge into

I take the path from

PERSONAE POEMS

In Latin, *persona* is the word for an actor's mask. Not a *literal* mask like the costumes you wore for Halloween when you were Superman, Snow White, or Frankenstein. But more of a character that can be tried on from the *inside*. Sort of like when you use the voice of someone *else* and present yourself to others *as this voice*. Think of the roles you play in your everyday life: the complaining tween who can lash out with major attitude: *As if. Give me a break.* The class clown who cracks jokes with her friends during recess. The serious student hunched over his desk, penciling answers onto a geography test.

When you get tired of talking about yourself, living *your* life, hearing the *I am, I have, I can, I want, I know* of all your beliefs, opinions, boasting achievements, that's the time to adopt a mask, or someone else's voice and point of view, for your own. Drop *your* story. Use this mask to speak *behind* and *from*. Slipping into and buttoning up a persona will allow you to express that which is difficult to say. Remember: in personae poems, it matters *less* what you're saying than *how* you're saying it. The poet David St. John has gone so far as to say that *as soon* as a poem gets to the page, it's *already* a persona.

Hi, My Name Is Rosa Parks

All I did was sit down
and it wasn't such a good seat either
just a seat.
All I did was sit down
and keep on sitting.
So what if a white man asked for my seat?
So what?
I got here first. It's mine.
The seat is mine.
And pretty soon all Blacks were saying it.
"This seat is mine."
"This seat is mine."
". . . and if you tell me otherwise,
I won't say it again.
I won't even try sitting down again."

So the white folks finally said the seat was ours.
The history books say it was me who caused it
but I don't think so.
It was all of us,
and it's not fair
for me to take all the credit.

Hi, my name's Rosa Parks
and all I did was sit down.

—Helen

Suddenly a Story.....

FRAGMENTS AND FIREWORKS

Claire wishes she could be hiking the Grand Canyon with her friends this vacation, all the way down to the Colorado, instead of picking lint off her sweater and watching her dog's paws twitch. A bag of chocolate-covered peanuts in the kitchen keeps calling her name, but her mom says to leave them until after dinner. Claire glances in the mirror and decides her hair, spiked and dyed green on top, resembles a cactus. The day is fading fast. The dog still needs a walk. Claire wrestles through her closet for a hat, feeling fragmented and lost. Outside, the know-it-all crows, *cawing* in their mocking way, arrive as a dare to Claire's ears to let go of her *poor-me-sorrow*. So she pulls on her lint-free sweater, drops the bag of chocolate-covered peanuts into her backpack, whistles for the dog, and heads down to the beach. Cars clog the road. The sand is damp. In the distance, a bonfire burns. Claire stops to ask a boy with kind eyes, "Hey, what's going on?" The dog leaps, tangling his leash around their legs. The boy laughs. Claire laughs, too. Fireworks light the sky. How could she have forgotten? It's the Fourth of July.

Story Starters

- Give yourself a new name and write about how you get from where you live to a place in nature—the beach, a park, a swing set. Mention what you bring along (a leash, choco-late-covered peanuts), and make up one person you meet along the way.
- Collect a few or a few hundred fragments about what you do or what someone else does that's typical, mundane, down-right boring (watching the dog's paws twitch). Combine a few into a paragraph *without* a tidy ending. Remind yourself that you're fine. Just as you are. Even when collecting lint off a sweater, even when writing in fragments.
- Let *not* writing be OK today. Don't sweat the small stuff and, as my friend Evan says, "Don't pet the sweaty stuff."

Your Turn

_____

_____

_____

_____

_____

_____

_____

_____

_____

_____

HAIR

Trust the universe and respect your hair.

—*Bob Marley*

As creative writers, we spend *a lot* of time *inside* our heads. All the more reason, I say, to relax our scalps. We have around a hundred thousand hair follicles on our head, so might I suggest picking up a brush *before* reaching for your pen today? Brushing—or *bruuushing* as a French friend calls it—can calm the part of the brain that's not needed when we meander down the page in search of a poem or story. Besides, a good brushing before writing can calm and distract the inner critic—who loves to give unasked-for advice—and keep his pointed presence distracted long enough to stay out of our spontaneous way. My inner critic *adores* a good *bruuushing*, and sometimes a neck and shoulder massage too.

While you're brushing, remember *all* the ways you've worn your hair. I didn't have any hair until I was two, so my mom taped a pink bow to my scalp while she figured out what to do. My hair did finally grow, and for a while I wore it long, tangled, and wild, collecting twigs, gum, and sap along each strand. My sister, cousin, and I used to play dress up with these ratty wigs my mother found at a flea market—I don't even want to think of *what* they were crawling with. "Rapunzel, Rapunzel, let down your golden hair!" we chanted, running through our tower bedrooms. In elementary school, I wore braids, pigtails, a pixie, a shag, even a style my Auntie Toots called a "Dorothy Hamill," after the famous Olympic figure skater. In junior high, I ventured into permanent waves, the bob, the rocker, and almost shaved my hair off entirely like my brave cousin Dawnie. I've used Mane 'n Tail, a horse shampoo, to thicken it, and rosemary oil—meant for cooking potatoes—to condition it. I've tucked my hair inside knit caps, twisted it into barrettes and rubber bands, piled it into nest-like updos, secured with sparkly clips. Come to think of it, I've plucked, tweezed, snipped, clipped, teased, and spent *way* too much time obsessing over my hair's shape, color, length, and texture. I mean, *jeez,* what's the big deal? Rastafarians regard their dreadlocks as "high-tension cables to heaven," but isn't hair just a bunch of threadlike strands of dead cells? Why not rebel already and leave it alone?

Tell me, what's up with *your* hair?

Drop Deeper

- What do you love *most* about your hair? What would you change? How would this make you feel?
- Describe a few ways—styles, colors, cuts—you've worn your hair.
- Write as though you are in that tower with Rapunzel, what would you say to her?
- Whose hair do you like to ruffle? How does it smell? (Like a maple-syrup-and-twig combo?)
- Offer a strand of your hair to the wind, your cat, a beloved aunt.

Hairs

Everybody in our family has different hair. My Papa's hair is like a broom, all up in the air. And me, my hair is lazy. It never obeys barrettes or bands. Carlos' hair is thick and straight. He doesn't need to comb it. Nenny's hair is slippery—slides out of your hand.

—Sandra Cisneros

Your Turn

DARES AND PEER PRESSURE

Through the white sun, Dawnie and I climb the path behind the house near the river. Down on the boat dock we place our towels side by side over the splintered planks. We slather Bain de Soleil suntan oil on each other's backs and shoulders and feel the heat soak into our skin, before rolling over into the bone-chilling water. No one is around to tell us what to do. Our parents are at work; my sister playing up the road with Jodie Olsen. School won't start for two more weeks. Dawnie looks over at me with that glint she sometimes gets before suggesting we do something sneaky.

"Let's try it, just once. So we'll know it's not for us." She has logic on her side. I know what she's referring to. We've talked about this. But I want to make her say it.

"Try what?"

"A cigarette."

"What if we get addicted?" I'm practical in my rule breaking.

"One puff. How can we?"

A water-skier passes behind a jet boat. Waves rock the dock.

"My dad keeps his with him," I explain.

"We can find butts from the ashtrays."

"Eew, gross."

We roll back into the water. Our hair hangs down like seaweed when we surface. Dawnie keeps her eyes closed. I stare at her dark lashes. We pull ourselves out and watch steam rise from where the water touches the boards of the dock. We wrap our towels around us, making them into sleeveless dresses. Up the rocky path, past the stone bench where I like to sit after my parents are asleep, we hike . . . past the deck where we'll pose for our last holiday photo, we climb. We hang out on the back steps until our bathing suits dry, then disappear through the sliding glass door into the empty house.

Slice of Your Life

- Find a few sentences about a time you snuck something with a friend. Wait to mention what was snuck until the *end* of your memoir-sketch.
- What do you consider a mistake? How do you know when you're making one?
- What's something you've done that you'd like to undo?
- Where did you swim as a child? Take me there on the page.

Your Turn

STREAM OF CONSCIOUSNESS

Stream of consciousness is writing that's automatic, spontaneous, and filled with free association. It's a style of writing where you don't hold *anything* back. You blurt it all out, whatever *it* is. Whatever's on your mind flows directly onto the stream of the page, as you let yourself swim in that choppy current, margin to margin, and hang on for dear life. You get to take off your life jacket and forget *all* ironbound rules relating to sentence structure, punctuation, and proper writing etiquette.

Stream of consciousness lets you catch your thoughts in *whatever* way they dive or dog-paddle through you. Meanwhile, with your trusty pen, you attempt to keep up. Broken bits of sad, mad, sassy, not yet fully born or about-to-die-trying thought-fragments and daydreams are *all* invited to share space on the page. André Breton, the leader of the Surrealist movement in Paris in the 1920s, instructed writers to "Write quickly, with no preconceived subject, so quickly that you retain nothing and are not tempted to reread. Continue as long as you please." Jack Kerouac, who lived in my neighborhood while writing *The Dharma Bums*, said it this way: "Take control and let loose." Besides being good advice for creative writing, Jack's advice can apply to other aspects of life too, like dancing, doodling, picking plums, and washing dishes. Sound easy? Try it.

Here's what might happen while you experiment with stream of consciousness writing: your handwriting could get shaky; your heartbeat might increase; your thoughts could let go of *all* logic. You might wonder, *Hey, is this OK?* (It is.) You might find friendly shark thoughts *and* vicious fish tricks share that vast ocean in there, with you.

Stream of Consciousness

Stream of consciousness? I can't write that fast. I can't even think that fast. My stream of consciousness is faster than the speed of light. I hate this place. Who says I have to stay in school? I hate following laws I didn't make. Brian got a haircut. He looks like a dandelion. Have you ever seen a haircut look like a flower? My friend Nate looks like he's wearing a carnation on his head. A big blonde carnation. Once I had a mother and a father. Now I have a mother. Now I have a father. But I don't have a mother AND a father. I talk to my mom when I forget she's gone. I wonder if she can hear me over three thousand miles of land. She wants to know why I never call or write. Mom, I say, I talk to you all the time. It's not my fault you don't listen. On Thursday I went for a walk. I brought along a cigarette and a stick of incense, but I had no lighter. I sat on the tire swings at Edna Maguire School and sang my mother's lullabies. I must have sung "You Are My Sunshine" at least six times. "You don't miss me," she says. "It's a bad connection," I reply. "I didn't hear what you just said." Mr. Gaynor is blinding today. I think it must be his shirt. What's it like to be deaf?

—Claire

YOUR MOODY MONKEY MIND

Don't let your head hijack your heart.

—James Higgins

Make a snack, pack a drink, find a pen, grab a notebook. Seek out a quiet place by a stream, at a park, on a swing, even in your old neighbor Jack's yard to sit and daydream. Then buckle your seat belt and prepare to let whatever's hanging around the vast interior of your mind *loose*. That's right, let the scrawl of the *who, what, where, why, when, how* of your mind's one-of-a-kind movements explode, go wild, *without* making them tame. Warning: what you write could get rude, crude, wild, true. It's OK. I'm encouraging you to bear witness to *all* your moods.

The mind is like a monkey, always leaping from thought-branch to thought-branch. Yours might be a comparing, judging, informing little monkey today. Or a tempting, provoking mongo screecher, who convinces you to leave your writing life *far* behind. (Like mine just did.) Maybe your monkey's clever today, insisting in a teasing way: *All your friends are out doing something fun, except for you. They're doing the most fun thing on the planet, and you're not with them.* My monkey likes to peer-pressure me to drop my pen and find excitement somewhere—*anywhere*—else. That's OK. Just notice that's what your mind's up to, nod your head, smile, and keep writing.

This monkey (our mind) is what we must name, tame, befriend, and really get to know, in order to feel comfortable in our skin. When we do this, we can write about anything *and* everything. Moving a pen across a page has always helped me with the calming and taming part. But I won't lie: it can be a *wild* storm in the middle of a vast jungle in there, before the calm kicks in. And it takes *bucket loads* of patience, risk, courage, and sometimes chocolate-covered bananas to watch your one-of-a-kind mind and *not* believe everything it thinks is true. Monkeys (our minds) like to play cerebral voodoo. They'll hijack our hearts, if we let them. Our job: *don't* let them! That's why I suggested the seat belt, in case you're wondering.

After sitting for a few minutes, jot down all the mind gossip that your monkey is attempting to convince you of. You might need to catch the gossip in fragments. (I do.) Then go call a friend and invite him to join you in writing all his mind gossip down. Writing like this with a friend is fun. Don't spread the gossip, though; let it go, rip it up, celebrate what you leave behind over a banana split.

Drop Deeper

- Use as many words around the word *mind* as you want, and jump into your monkey's right-now rhythm. Use white space for more pause around the gossip of your thoughts. It's OK to leave a trail of ink *outside* the margins.
- Compose a Who-What-Where-When-Why-How mind poem like Natalie did (on the following page).

- together apart together mind   stop the clock and catch that
- ball   say it's all right to make it all up mind   write that poem
- with flower-power mind   whatever you do don't let this life
- pass you by mind   I miss you and your listening eyes like crazy
- mind   and here I am creating a temple in the forest of my mind
- traveling deeper into my forever one of a kind mind   where
- everything's been   and always will be   sweet sassy ripe wild
- heart pried-open mind.

Who can find their way through a maze
of black roses? What bird lands
on my shoulder every day?
Where do I find an underground
world with an open window?
When will a bouquet of conjoined
hands knock on my door?
Why can't my own mouth leave my face?
How, oh how, will X-ray vision
affect my poet-mind's eyesight?

—Natalie

Your Turn

YOUR HEART'S FIRST HUNCH

A hunch is creativity trying to tell you something.

—*Frank Capra*

Let your heart's *first* hunch or inkling be what guides you through this next survey. Swap head-logic for heart-logic. The only requirement: be willing to "allow for strangeness," as poet Jane Hirshfield suggests. Don't play it safe. Dare to write something you've *never* written before, go *beyond* one-word answers, and leave your fear of being wrong in the dust with your eraser. There never is and never will be a "right" way to create, so celebrate by taking your heart and imagination out for a date. After this survey, choose any part of what you wrote to compose a ten-line poem. Fool around with word order, take words out, toss them back in, recombine images until your bright-eyed heart's totally satisfied. Bottom line: make up your *own way* to play on the page today.

If speech is a mouth, silence is like

a thread of peace or the edge of forgetting, where an ache lingers or a fern unfurls; the way the blue distance shatters into orange; how all this space inside the heart center gets befriended, absorbed.

・
・
・
・
・
・

Legs take us up the stairs, the heart leads us toward

_____

_____

Strength is friends with

_____

_____

Days change into _____

_____

Each season dances like _____

_____

The heart dreams of_____

_____

I'm chasing words that begin with S (choose any letter):

_____

_____

The heart hooks together swift things like _____

_____

The page ignites with lightning-in-a-bottle–like moments like

_____

_____

The sky is where I keep/find/lose/toss (circle one) _____

_____

No matter how tired, my life keeps racing toward

_____

_____

THE LYRIC ESSAY

I n a lyric poem, you attempt to create an emotional experience of a single moment. Daydreaming, say, while looking out the window during fifth-period algebra, imagining yourself down at the creek skipping stones. Sort of like a snapshot, lyric poems are short and songlike and express the thoughts *and* feelings of the poet. No stories with characters allowed. Exploratory essays let you pass through unknown territory of time and space to find your way *toward* and *into* your own unique truth. Add the two together and you have—*sha-zam*—a lyric essay, which is also called a "poetic essay" or "essayistic poem."

What's great about lyric essays is that they don't require narrative, or even logic. (That sound is me shouting *Hip hip hooray!* Logic can be *so* overrated.) Lyric essays welcome the strange *and* the imaginative, allow for gaps in thought, and are a *preferred* form for short attention spans. (Like mine.) They move by association from one thought-path to another, side-winding snakelike or leaping poem-like as they circle a single image. The lyric essay doesn't explain itself. It doesn't have to. It doesn't confess. Why should it? *Well, then what does it do?* you ask. It dances. It trusts. It lets the reader guess. It's *mysterious.*

To write a lyric essay, start by taking a few facts, then merge them together to describe an object, a moment in time, a person in relation to a spot in nature. Focus on that oval-shaped stone you found crossing the creek. The one you tucked into your pocket. Or the turbocharged darkness outside your window. Or a friend's ankle bracelet. The voice of the lyric essay has been likened to one you "overhear and feel close to, even if you can't exactly see who's speaking." Y-o-u get to create and *become* this voice. How cool is that?

You'll pass over a few bumps. You will. Weave around others. Tattered longing is part of the ride. Woven webs. A few candle-lit lanterns. The hero of your journey has always been you. With shoulder-length hair. You play a mean game of cards. Wield a quick knife. Toss a few stones. A river flows. From the beginning, you've never been lost.

—group poem

I show her the way from a fragment into a few steps. We search for Canada's evening sky by looking inward to black and white. Art in bloom sends inspiration. Light blasts through something new. Internal forces breathe. At the holiday party, her ankle bracelet smells like lemons. Forced into a churning heartbeat, we shovel away all grief.

—David (Tem)

CIRCLES

The whole universe is based on rhythms.
Everything happens in circles, in spirals.

—John Hartford

D ream up words or phrases to widen the definition of a circle. Then peer in or dare to step inside as you name *everything* you can imagine that tastes, smells, sounds, feels, looks round or elliptical *to you*. Ponder possibilities. Take liberties. Your circle imagery need not make head sense. My friend Cathy's list includes a cupcake's bottom, an opera singer's mouth, a jumpy exclamation mark (Oh, my!). Find *your* circle rhythm and keep adding to this list, squeezing circle-like images into any white-space vacancy below. Spiral closer to your own brand of magical roundness, minus any dizziness. Or circle ten images you like from my list on the next page. Hint: Your circle answers can float in the realm of the rational and the *non*rational today.

A soap bubble
C.'s soccer ball
The outer rim of Joan's teacup
The letter *O*
Your left nostril
My right nostril
The eye of a squirrel
A cloud formation
Your belt loop
A blueberry
The freckle below my thumb
A pimple
A barnacle
A raisin in the sun
Carolyn's wedding ring
An owl's hoot
A Hula-Hoop
An egg yolk
A Ferris wheel
The clock in the yoga room
A grape
A smoke ring
A wolf's midnight howl
J's burp from the back row
A car's steering wheel
Erin's sunglasses
Duke's dog collar
A pebble
A prayer bead

Jenna's bracelet
The first syllable of Olivia's name
The inside of a sunflower
The earth's orbit
The moon's reflection
A short story
A polka dot
A dime, penny, nickel, quarter
Love given
Love received
A hug
A grain of sand
That speck of oatmeal on your chin
A shot of longing
The creek's ripple
An oak's acorn
A planet or two
A lost echo
A boomerang's trajectory
The pink cosmos
The sound of "pop"
A spiderweb's gossamer center
A peephole
A doorknob
A moon rock
An igloo
A mound of clay from Carin's studio
Your belly button
A flamingo's eyes

CIRCLE DANCE

There is nothing so wise as a circle.

—Rainer Maria Rilke

Use the Untie Your Mind List from the previous chapter (see page 50) to write about finding *your* way *inside* a circle. Claim your space in the center of your imagination, make a full turn, and pile on *any* and *all* circlelike-image combinations until you have nothing more to say within the maze of allotted space.

Go on, invite someone into a circle with you. What will you do? Write *around* the edge of the page? Layer sight *and* sound images? Gaze at the pink cosmos through a shot of longing or the lens of a flamingo's eye? Swirl into that whip of air in a boomerang's trajectory . . . nibble the hole of a glazed doughnut? Maybe you'll make circular sentences using only similes. Maybe your circle-journey will include a few squares. For advanced circle-dancers: select five of your most original images and turn them into a meandering poem you're proud to take home and claim as your own.

If I invited you into a circle . . .

We would

- count echoes and slow dance and sip orange tea with honey.
- We'd eat Oreos and write poems about wide-eyed owls who soar
- through the dark outside my tree-house window. We'd howl at the
- moon, walk the trail that loops through town, and, starting over
- again, invite all our friends to join in.

Look inside for _____

Gaze at _____

Reach for _____

Count _____

Grasp _____

Swirl into _____

Dance with _____

Share _____

Hold gratitude for _____

Release _____

DAYDREAM BELIEVER

I have never let my schooling interfere with my education.
—Mark Twain

"So there was this poet," the teacher begins, "who was sent into a room to write everything he knew for sure about himself on one side of a piece of paper . . . and on the other side, a list of everything he didn't yet know." End of May, with only two weeks left of school, Alex can't keep his mind from wandering. Warm air laced with wisteria drifts in to find him in the back row, by the window . . . and, all at once, he's off hiking the hill behind the middle school with his buddy Eric, shooting the breeze and razzing each other the way good friends do. One second, he's in that stuffy classroom, the next he's heading across the soccer pitch, on his way home to see his dog and invent a new way to link a series of haiku. He's starting to figure out that his deepest truths live inside of him, along with all of his answers to everything and that, sometimes, his imagination has to drift out and away from what his teachers expect him to say. He's learning to trust the strength of his intuition and sturdy instincts. Trust that true light of knowing that lives as a permanent resident in his heart center, a place that

years of schooling often attempt to erase. So when the teacher
clears his throat and calls on him, asking, "Alex, are you paying
attention?" he looks up and answers that he most definitely is.

Story Starters

- Our deepest truths *always* contain both sides. Like the dark side and the light side of the moon. Write *toward* discovering both sides of a truth or story. Finish these sentences: Here's what I know for sure: _____.
Here's what I don't yet know: _____.
(Don't let the end of the line stop you. Keep alternating between I know, I don't know, I know, I don't know . . . as you write *off* the page.)
- What do you care most about? Who taught you to care?
- A guy named Socrates said, "Wisdom begins in wonder." A guy named Shakespeare said, "These are but wild and whirling words." Track where your mind wanders during class, and see if you can turn your wonderings into a daydream-type story with wild and whirling words. Begin with the last thing your teacher said.

Your Turn

DOODLE DOWN

My hobbie . . . is using a lot of scotch tape . . . to pick out different things during what I read and piece them together and [make] a little story of my own.

—*Louis Armstrong*

Hard as I tried, I could not understand a thing Ms. Bowen said or embrace her love of historical facts and dates. Sitting in the second row behind Todd Cooper, I *longed* for her words to paint a story in my mind though they rarely did. I didn't know yet that it was through pictures, metaphors, poetry, music, and stories that I had to learn about the world. I didn't know yet that I was the type of kid who needed to gaze out windows and use the dreaming, doodling side of my brain to perceive my life . . . that this part of me was *as important* as breathing. I didn't know yet how deeply I felt my feelings, and those of everyone else in the room, too. So I just kept memorizing those facts and dates Ms. Bowen spouted and got good grades, though I couldn't remember a thing after taking the test. I wanted to learn something true about myself, but didn't know yet that I needed to scotch tape a few pictures and feelings together in order to surprise myself and learn what I truly longed for.

Sometimes now, when I visit a school, I turn out the lights, sit on the floor, and invite a new group of students to join me for a doodle while we're getting to know one another. This relaxes me—and anyone else who might need a vantage point closer to the earth in order to listen, hear, and feel a little deeper, before making a word-world of their own. I understand that sitting in our desks, paying attention, and having the right answers to questions asked are a *big* part of succeeding in school. It's just that with shoes off, sitting cross-legged, with a blank sheet of paper and a favorite pen, I feel calmer, less guarded, and better equipped to find my way *into* what's most true for me. (What about you?)

Thinking isn't always necessary to write a poem. You can also fool around with words and doodle into your heart-space to compose a few lines of magic. Today, I'm into spirals and stars, lightning bolts, pyramids, lopsided hearts, and sideways figure eights. Even the shy and often overlooked dot, a favorite of my poet-pal Prartho, makes an appearance:

Today, a dot becomes the green marble of my cat's left eye, the only cloud in the April sky, the last Rice Krispie survivor at the bottom of my cereal bowl, the center of forgiveness, a ladybug's spot, a lost raindrop, the high note that ends a song, the doorknob we all turn to get into this room.

What's a dot or the mysterious letter *O* look like to you? Doodle a few and find out.

Drop Deeper

- Fill an *entire* page with doodles: peace signs, stars, swirls, tight whirling tornados, sparks at the tip of a firecracker. *Any random doodle you can imagine putting into a poem.*
- Write *to* or about: the shape of your soul, the sky's first star,

a startled lightning bolt, a lost hieroglyphic. Scotch tape two
doodles together and decide what they equal. Or write *to* the
insistent exclamation mark, a confused question mark, those
three stuttering ellipses . . .

- Ask your favorite doodle a question. (Hey, what's the differ-
ence between a squiggle and a doodle anyway?) Get lost inside your asking.

The spiral's the mess of my room. A spark
flaming wider, taking on greater force.
How the world instantly ends, then begins
again and again and again.

An ellipsis equals the wheels of a train
plowing into the next sentence
or three calls of a fatherless bird.

—Julian

How is the soul shaped?
Like an unknown color inside
a raindrop that makes up a cloud.
The seed hidden within a lonely tulip.
A sentence of forgiveness
or a path that leads to a place called home.
The invisible proton that holds together
a friendship so it will never end.

—Libby

Your Turn

Surprise Yourself Survey

BUBBLES OF FLAVORS, TASTES, AND SCENTS

One of the real tests of writers, especially poets,
is how well they write about smells.

—Diane Ackerman

Taste signals stick together with smell signals in the *same* part of our brain. That's why it's hard to enjoy a peanut butter brownie when you have a stuffy nose or head cold. We need *both* senses to get the fullness of each flavor. Salty like barbecue potato chips, sour like a lime, sweet like a ripe strawberry, zesty like tomato salsa, spicy like a green chili, sweet *and* sour like a tangerine.

Finish the lines on the next page that describe flavors, tastes, or scents that you feel like exploring. To carry you deeper into your personal definition, use words, memories, similes, and textures that have *nothing* whatsoever to do with food. Cover an entire page with bubbles and leave plenty of empty space inside for your flavor, taste, scent answers to puff up and expand. "But what if I like diamonds, ovals, or parallelograms?" you ask. Well, then draw some of those instead.

Lemons and light remind me of

Nana's hugs, and how she'd tuck me into sheets filled with the
sunshine pulled off her clothesline and tell me she loved me more
than tongue can tell.

Freedom smells like _____

The flavor of the moon is ripe with _____

_____

Too much homework tastes chalky like_____

Safety smells warm like _____

_____

Here's the smell of my dad's head when I'd sit sit on his shoulders

_____

Ripe peaches and creek sounds bring me back to_____

_____

Loneliness includes the scent of _____

A kiss near the ocean tastes like _____

_____

Fireflies and a moonless night smell like _____

_____

Pine sap and burned marshmallows remind me of _____

_____

The flavor of Monday morning is _____

_____

The taste of Friday afternoon is like _____

_____

Hint

- Step closer to scent and taste through the side door of feelings. A kiss near the ocean can taste like shy excitement. The feeling of missing someone can be humid and sneak up on you like hunger . . .

FIRST DAY

No one can possibly know what is about to happen: it is happening, each time, for the first time, for the only time.

—James Baldwin

How many times have you said, "Oh, I remember the first time: *I met you* . . . *played with* . . . *discovered* . . . *tasted* . . . *visited* . . . *hiked* . . . *tried* . . . *heard* . . ."? Say one of these *I remember the first times* right now, out loud to yourself, or to a friend, or to the posts and beams in the room where you're sitting, holding this book for the very first time.

Firsts are important. Firsts are powerful. We tend to remember first times with *precise* detail, because we're meeting ourselves in a *brand-new* situation for the very first time, which naturally makes us feel more awake and filled with shimmering waves of curiosity and wonder. When we pay first-time kind of attention, we get to use our first-take observations later on, *on the page*.

Run back through a few first days, down the halls of a few favorite grades with a few favorite teachers, the arrival of your first brother or sister, the first time you learned the truth about your parents being Santa Claus (I hope I'm not the first to break the news), the first time you met a favorite friend, the first time you visited a favorite place on this planet or any other planet. What first wants to be explored first today?

Drop Deeper

- What's the first memory that sneaks up on you?
- Write the first thing you ate this morning—and where you ate it.
- Where's the first place you'd go if you were running away from home?
- What's the first thing you'd like to know about your future?

Wild Life

Hiking up that great wall of snowcapped peaks,
the path is edged with treasure.
This is the forever that goes unseen.
This is where I've come to be calm.
I'm tempted to curl up in the newly dewed grass.
Here for the first time, I think, *What a great place.*
This never-ending sea of green,
soon to be changed by human hands.
Am I seeing it for the last time?

—Kyler

Your Turn

FIRST PROMISE

I tape four pieces of construction paper side by side, spell WELCOME in black crayon, and hang the banner low against the stars of the front window. On Dad's leather chair, I wait—all the way back on worn leather—my legs resting over the edge, my hands in my lap folded neatly. The night my mother brings my new sister home and cradles her down to me, I move the warm blanket back and memorize the shape of her head, studying the lines of her new skin. I want her to know me, hear her voice sing my name. This weight I hold is our beginning.

Later, beside the slatted crib, I stand, whispering—as soon as her hair grows, I promise to wash and braid it the way I do all my dolls. I promise to teach her the songs I'm learning from Mrs. Chamberlin in kindergarten, to make her a cake in my Easy-Bake Oven. I explain how she'll sleep with me when thunder roars, so we can count our heartbeats.

Only then, I pretend the electricity really *does* flicker off. "I *have* to carry you to safety," I whisper standing over her bassinet. So I steady myself and—hanging on tight down the dark hall—I accidentally bump her softness against the rough wall, where she makes a shy sound like when I get scared. Afraid she'll wake up, I can't let my parents know something is wrong, so I lean my face down to my new baby and feel her warm breath against my cheek. "I promise," I say. "Next time I'll be more careful." But she only scrunches her mouth, raises her tiny hands to her face, and, with fingernails that look like diamonds, rubs her blue eyes back to sleep. All by myself I've carried her. Doesn't this mean she belongs to me?

Slice of Your Life

- Write about a time you obviously went too far.
- Finish this line: *This is what can happen when . . .*

_____

_____

- Write about making (or breaking) a promise. Somewhere use the word *lightning, diamond,* or *fingernails.*

Your Turn

THE TRAP OF NOTHING

I am so busy doing nothing . . . that the idea of doing
anything—which as you know, always leads to something—
cuts into the nothing and forces me to have to drop everything.

—*Jerry Seinfeld*

Do you ever feel bombarded with inquiring questions about
your life? *What are you doing? Where are you going? Who
are you hanging out with?* Do you ever get tired of answering with
dates and details? Ever wish your parents and teachers would drop
all their nosy concern and *chillax* already?

When you feel pelted by too many questions—like this one,
say— do you ever shrug, look in the other direction, and mumble
"Nothing"? (I've been known to do this, and then run down the
hall of my mind and slam a few doors behind me.) At times, we
all need the protection of *Nothing*, especially when we want a little space from so much *Everything*—math homework, chores, demands disguised as requests, all the growing-up stuff that keeps
piling up around us.

Reflect on what you do while hanging out in your own

mode of *Nothing*. Poke around between that mumbled *I dunno*. Investigate what's *underneath* your shrug. Rappel into the dark void of *Nothing*'s center and add a few word-knots of what you *don't* remember, didn't see or feel or think. Are you brave enough to meet the life force of Nothing, to face the truth of what Nothing might mean?

Drop Deeper

- What question do you so *not* want to be asked?
- Include why you *aren't* going to answer, who you *aren't* going to talk to, what you *aren't* going to speak, eat, catch, and release.
- What *isn't* in your heart, soul, fist, or hiding between the letters of your name today? Consider turning part of your investigative list into a poem like Janina did. Or not.

The Trap of Nothing

There's nothing
in my name's fist,
not a popcorn kernel,
not a key, not a guppy,
poison oak leaf or strand of hair.
Not Barbie sunglasses
or a piece of plankton, or ants—
not the hottest coal.
No, not even a raindrop
if you must know.
There's Nothing—In fact,
I almost named myself Nothing.
Zip, Nada, No way, Forget about it.

I don't think so. Just turn around
and never come back.

—Janina

My Soul

Not dew
not a silvery spiderweb
not an astronaut in space
not a gurgly potion
not a silky mist
not even a piece of paper—
but the life that is inside of me.

—Charlie

Your Turn

_____

_____

_____

_____

_____

_____

_____

_____

LET NATURE TAKE THE LEAD

In-Just- / spring when the world is mud- / luscious . . .
/ when the world is puddle-wonderful.
—e.e. cummings

As a writer, nature can be one of your *best* friends. Especially when you need a break from talking, explaining, answering questions, making sense. Pick three words from the next page: combine the first two words using "and," then tack on the third word using "of."

• • • *The* drumming ebb *and* flow *of* stillness.

Keep going and show where this image in nature "leads."

• • • • *leads me into a night journey of green-footed wonder where I scale the walls of fear and drop to the other side, into the "puddle-wonderful" of the world.*

See how many words you can combine into images. Pack along this advice by the poet Wallace Stevens: "A poem need not have a meaning and, like most things in nature, often does not."

rain
snow
ebb and flow
mud
sunburned
sky
mist
sacred
stream
green
sparks
elms
autumn
minnows
trail
earth
storm
fern
drifts
stillness
fire
river
night
ablaze
grass
trout

rock
forest
moss
roots
air
moose
downpour
iced over
oaks
rumbling
jagged
fog
redwoods
sand
dewdrops
shade
cattails
shadows
moonlight
lake
rapids
foam
summer
clouds
damp
windy

spring
humming
trails
stars
lightning
meadow
journey
echo
canyon
curling
pine
drought
harvest
footprints
flow
picnic
fox
howl
rabbit
mountain
ridges
stones
thunder
mosquito
owl
frost

BLUE HOUR

Only from the heart / Can you touch the sky.
—Jalaluddin Rumi

W hat color are you in love with this hour? If you're not sure, take a walk to a paint store and peek at those small, square color samples. Pick out a few to tuck into your pockets. (The paint store makes them for you.) On your way home, stop by the drugstore and check out the names on bottles of nail polish and lip gloss, or find a box of Crayola crayons. With names like *Atomic Tangerine, Hog Wild Red, Banana Berry Blitz,* and *Bittersweet Shimmer,* you might want to have a pen and index card handy.

For many moons, I've been in love with every shade of blue. July sky blue, underwater blue, cornflower blue, ultramarine, turquoise, lapis lazuli. (Just saying lapis lazuli makes me swoon.) I learned from a poet named Carolyn Forché that in French, *l'heure bleue,* or "the blue hour," is the light between darkness and day, a clear, in-between, hovering hour when our senses wake up. An hour we get to greet every morning if we're not lost in dream or hibernating in our warm cave of sleep. Each blue hour casts a light like no other. True blue, baby blue, straining through winter sun blue. . . .

What hour is like no other for you? High noon? Lunchtime? Just before bed? Late at night when everyone's under their quilt of dreams again? We only have a certain number of these hours, hovering or not, in our one lifetime. No need to fret, just locate the color—and the hour—that *most* inspires you. You'll find, hear, feel *endless* ways to describe it sooner or later. Add words *before* (and *after*) to give your color heft and meaning.

Here's my sooner-or-later list:

- *lion dance blue, crack and ripple blue, into the wild blue yonder, quiet*
- *along the blue road to freedom, know-it-all blue, long distance and*
- *still wanting to talk to you blue.*

Then dig out a poem, story, or memoir segment, and search for opportunities to drip or swirl in your expanded color hues.

Drop Deeper

- How does your color move? Does it *hover, skip, crawl, shuffle, slide,* or *shift* its shape? (You can pick your own verbs.) With whom and where does your color travel? What memory does it share? Does it talk back? What in nature does it leap over, slide under, scatter, or blend into? What sound does it lean toward? What happens when you hold it in your hands and stroke its back? What else about your color wants to be heard, witnessed, shared, or remain hidden?

A Rush of Blue

A rush of blue streams in
quick and calm—
the feeling is so great;
the Earth returns to blue,

the trees and roads
feel it coming on
and instantly they, too, turn
into blue—suddenly
everything blue.

—Collin

Your Turn

_____

_____

_____

_____

_____

_____

_____

_____

_____

_____

_____

_____

_____

EARLY RISER

If it's your job to eat a frog, it's best to do it first thing
in the morning.

—Mark Twain

Be honest. Have you *ever* gotten up (willingly) before the sun for the sole purpose of watching the sky wake up? If not, set the alarm clock for 5 A.M. (Yes, really.) You owe it to yourself to do some things in life at least *once*. Resist the urge to hit the snooze button. Roll over and find the quickest route out of bed. Zip on a fleece jacket, bring along your blanket, hug your pillow. Stop by the bathroom, then find your way outside for a view of the sky. Whatever you do, *don't* close your eyes. *Do* be a witness, though, as the sun turns the key to open the day. Listen for crickets, birds, any near or faraway sounds: wind caught in tree limbs, a sprinkler's hiss, that backing-up garbage truck, your stomach's hunger-rumbles. Feel the sticky drizzle. Find out what it's like to live *inside* early morning's brevity as light breaks through all that dark disappearing before you.

Emily Dickinson must have been an early riser, since she wrote, "I'll tell you how the Sun rose— / A Ribbon at a time—." Let yourself be guided deeper into something bigger than who you think you are, as you scribble fragments about *your* early morning life. And if you absolutely *can't* wake up at dawn? Then make a date to watch the sky's light fade its firey good-bye, tallying how many shades of pink and orange you can detect, name, add to the cloud of the page.

Drop Deeper

- Write three colors you enjoy saying or using in your writing (jazzberry jam, robin's-egg blue, origami orange). Then find three things you trust that match each color. Combine one thing from each list. Fine to make up colors. Fine to make up what you trust.

I trust my heartbeat and jazzberry jam, the rise and fall of my cat's warm belly and his love of robin's-egg blue; I trust wide-eyed wonder and another day to play as I feed my hunger of folding origami and locating that mystery word that rhymes with orange.

- Stay in bed after being woken and sing the blues like Dylan did. Be sure to use plenty of whining and repetition. Who wants you out of bed? What gets said as you're woken up? What's your response?

Blues

Oh, she woke me up in the morning.
She said, "Get out of bed."
Oh, she woke me up in the morning.
She said, "Get out of bed."

And let me tell you that waking up
gets to my head.

I said, "No, no, I wanna sleep.
I wanna stay away from the mornin' heat."
Oh, she woke me up in the mornin'.
She said, "Get out of bed."

And let me tell you that wakin' up
gets to my head.

—Dylan S.

Your Turn

_____

_____

_____

_____

_____

_____

_____

_____

_____

_____

IN EVERY HOUSE

There ought to be a room in every house to swear in.

—Mark Twain

Locate your favorite room or a place *within* a room (your bed, the end of the couch, the warm spot on the floor by the dryer). It might even be the last room you swore in. Then list three words you associate with this room *and* three things that have *nothing* to do with this room. Like a snappy mood you're in, or a summer memory, a type of weather, part of a song lyric, the make and model of your favorite car, and so on. For example, if you picked *kitchen,* you might write: *wooden spoons, cinnamon sticks, wobbly table* (all items you'd find in my kitchen). You might also write: *a warm rain, riding bareback, a pickup soccer game* (things you wouldn't necessarily find in my kitchen but are unique to my life).

Combine and tweak your two lists, using the handy connecting words *of, and,* or *with its,* to create sentences that your ears like the pace and feel of. (FYI: You can't do this wrong!) "In my kitchen of cinnamon sticks and rain, wooden spoons and my dream of riding a horse named Gypsy bareback, I sit at my breakfast table with the wobbly legs and remember that pickup soccer game I wish I'd had sense enough to skip." Assemble your three favorite rooms or your entire house.

Kitchen	Backyard	Hallway
Garage	Family room	Mudroom
Bed	Entryway	Mailbox
Attic	Closet	Roof
Front porch	Swimming pool	Bathroom
Window seat	Firewood cubby	Basement
Living room	Bathtub	Dining room
Stairwell	Tree house	Shower

HAIBUN

aibun were developed in Japan in the seventeenth century by Matsuo Munefusa, a poet who went by the name Bashō. A haibun combines prose *and* haiku to create a prose-poem that focuses on the reporting of everyday moments from *your* everyday life. Haibun are fun and flexible enough to hold leaps of thoughts *and* feelings. They can be like a little story that's full of emotion, that leads to an understanding about yourself, a place, another person, or a thing, like a shaky breeze or the sound of leaving.

Haibun are inspired by *paying attention* to nature, simple objects, a story, or a journey. They can be written in fragments and might include autobiography, biography, diary, essay, and even your day and night dreams. They can range from a few lines to a book full of fluttering pages. Think of haibun as *mininarratives*. Moments in a life (yours) that *show* rather than tell. Things and details—this *showing* of a life—are what our imaginations are hungry *and* thirsty for. Use the haibun's container to hold a stream of sensory impressions—sight, taste, smell, sound, touch words—that arrive to your eyes, mouth, nose, ears, fingertips, and heart *directly* from your ordinary life outside or inside your classroom, before or after poetry like Lou Lou and Will did. You can locate a haibun by walking along the sidewalk, stopping to notice a flower, or minding your own business. They are anywhere and everywhere, waiting for your attention.

Haibun are written in the *present tense,* to make it seem like the experience is unfolding *right now.* Sentences are short, and you get to tack on a haiku at the end, like a little "punctuation mark of feeling," to travel *beyond* what you just reported. You remember haiku: those three short lines you wrote in third grade that capture a moment, just as it is. No similes or metaphors required. Just short line, long line, short line. (Skip the seventeen-syllable count, unless you're writing in Japanese.)

If you're attempting your first haibun, go slow, feel your way in. Give yourself permission to get close to your life. (It is yours, after all!) With your hands on the handlebars, take a haibun for a ride. Or skip the haibun, and take a haiku-hike. No gear, no sunscreen, no explanations required.

Outside, early November, footsteps in back of me. Birds chirp like they need to find a home. Kids surround me, writing poems about what's around them. Sun shifts from sunny to doomy. Every second a rainbow is about to start. The boys practice memorizing their states on the black pavement. I forget about the test.

wind coming down—
a shaky breeze
lost in the middle

—Lou Lou

Lightning sparks speed through moonlight shining into the misty distance. The rocky ground burns. Flickering light whirls in my mind. A magic-fragment trickles through a stream, heading to the ocean. Dew-drips form on my sharpened pencil. The weedy creek trembles down the green hill of my imagination.

the sound of leaving
at the end
of Poetry.

—Will

Hint

- When you write haiku, remember to find words that *re-create* the experience of an emotion rather than describe it. I remember it like this: Haiku are *best* when you *suggest*.

Suddenly a Story . . . .

HAPPINESS AND THE SOUND OF GEESE

Wandering around her life, Gen flops down after school on the futon in her friend Jeff's living room. A path of sunlight filters through an open window. Jeff, who likes asking questions, wonders what sound today makes Gen the happiest. Right then, a flock of geese begins honking. A feathered beating of wings flaps above Parker Street. In the field of Jeff's front yard, bees buzz in their velvety bodies. Gen listens to her heart's steady *da-Dum, da-Dum* as a cloud of exhaustion lifts and, in a flash, it's *Hello happiness.* Gen feels the gratitude of a Friday afternoon bubble up like the fizz from her root beer and knows, though she can't exactly explain *how,* everything in her life—from her allergy over algebra to her ailing grandmother—is going to be all right. Waving good-bye to Jeff, she takes a new route home, and wonders what else makes her happy. Turns out, wondering and wandering are high on her list. The tangerine she pulls from her backpack tastes happy. The scent of eucalyptus and wood smoke smells happy. Seeing her poetry teacher, who stops to say *Hi* in front of the library . . . there it is again. Happiness, practically grazing her shirtsleeve.

Story Starters

- Just notice what you notice. Record anything that catches your ears' attention and causes the corners of your mouth to soften upward. The lyrics from a song, a friend's reckless laugh, your neighbor's dog barking his joy at the passing world, even the fizzy upward-floaty bubble sound from your root beer.
- Take a mini inventory of what quirky things your friends like to do. (Eric likes walking in the rain without an umbrella; Ali collects orange traffic cones; Michelle dances through her living room in ballet shoes.) Expand on what one friend likes to do writing from his or her point of view. (*Become* that friend.)
- Fill in the blanks: Happiness tastes of _____ with a hint of the sound of _____ and with light like _____; it's the scent of _____ and the feel of _____. So there.

Your Turn

WABI-SABI

To understand *wabi-sabi,* it's said you have to grasp that beauty is *not* in the object—a fistful of dandelions, the sound of geese—but in *your experience of it:* the feeling-meaning, the mood, or the atmosphere it brings up *inside you.*

Wabi-sabi is hard to pin down. Even the Japanese don't try to define it, and it originated in Japan! Wabi-sabi isn't limited to art or what's found in nature. It can be the *magic* of *paying attention* to *everyday things.* Dust particles rising from the couch you just flopped on, a snail's oozy trail, that avocado pit in a bowl of sludge you left on the windowsill from last month's science experiment. Wabi-sabi has *everything* to do with the *quality* of attention that you bring to what you see.

To experience wabi-sabi for yourself: TAKE a less-is-more mind-set. SEEK out what's been here all along. NOTICE yourself noticing what you're noticing. (Harder than it sounds.) TURN *toward* what's unique, imperfect, flawed. FOLLOW an unmarked trail *deeper in.* FIND a special beauty all your own in some unexpected place. Yes, even a slightly dark memory place. RESPECT how *everything* will continue to change and change (and change). Walk through an empty lot or sit among a patch of weeds. Put yourself in close proximity to a messy room (you may not have to walk far) or offer to take out the garbage and dare yourself to find at least one thing that helps you understand wabi-sabi along the way. Hint: When seeking out what's wabi-sabi, the smaller, the better.

Between Walls

the back wings
of the

hospital where
nothing

will grow lie
cinders

in which shine
the broken

pieces of a green
bottle

—William Carlos Williams

Before School

My son steps
on a snail—
I hear the shell
crush beneath
his shoe.
Through the window,
I watch him
on the ground
examine
the clear ooze.

—Karen

SCENTS AND STONES

People have often told me that one of their strongest childhood memories is the scent of their grandmother's house.

—Adriana Trigiani

My friend Christopher has been a "nose" person since he was a kid. Scents seemed magical to him, because they conjured up feelings and memories that he could only "visit" via the sense of smell. Like honeysuckle, which to him is that glittering hour of twilight and those boundless days of summer in the woods behind his house in East Longmeadow, Massachusetts. He was fascinated by the idea that when he smelled something, he was taking in minute particles of that *thing*. Honeysuckle's sweetness = connections with family and friends. Lilac = night and the wistful delicacy of childhood. Drawn to the scents of flowers, Christopher studied aromatherapy, and soon was creating special scent-blends while working for a company that made candles. Certain scents, he learned, just make us more calm, others more excited. What scents calm or excite *you*? (Maybe go sniff a flower or a candle to find out.)

Pick a stone and scent that you think sound good together (or create some made-up combos) and include them in a fragrant sentence. You might combine your birthstone and a scent from your grandmother's house, and put them into an ode to childhood. The deep purple of amethyst and the scent of tree sap take me back to Nana's house on Kirk Avenue, picking figs in her backyard at dusk, and sharing the day's story.

Stones

Hawk's-Eye	Larimar	Yellow Jade
Amethyst	Turquoise	Moonstone
Labradorite	Staurolite	Amazonite
Opal	Rose Quartz	Garnet
Cat's-Eye	Smoky Quartz	Green Aventurine
Aquamarine	Ocean Jasper	White Jade
Amber	Green Jade	Blue Tigereye
Lapis Lazuli	Blue Lace Agate	Onyx

Scents

Lavender	Myrtle	Vanilla
Bergamot	Chamomile	White Peony
Vetiver	Lemon Verbena	Tuberose
Jasmine	Yarrow	Violet
Rose Geranium	Frankincense	Tree sap
Rose Otto	Ylang-Ylang	Tangerine
Sandalwood	Patchouli	Wild Mint

Tip

*   For more scents to choose from, take the survey on page 61.

345 GORDON AVENUE

Here's the house my father remodeled, with the Zen garden in the shade of four pine trees. The house that smelled of rosemary and garlic, where we hosted holiday parties and someone new sat at the table in the dining room each night, and spun the lazy Susan to reach the basket of homemade bread. The house where my parents rented a room to Helen, an opera singer from Maryland, who practiced Italian arias in the shower and my sister and I stood in the hall to listen. The house where Brother Richard stayed when he decided not to take his vows and become a priest, and where Mrs. Patnude arrived every Tuesday to give me piano lessons while Richard hid in the kitchen and baked brownies. The house where my mom's pal, Marty, ended her ten-mile run each Sunday, panting at the screen door, gulping water from the glass I handed her, then calling *Too-da-loo, Sweetie*. The house with the long flight of stairs that Kristin, Paisley, Betsy, and I took turns sliding down in a slippery orange sleeping bag, laughing when one of us crashed through the cat door at the bottom. The house where my cousin Dawnie and I ate olives off our fingertips and roller-skated on the checkered linoleum in the family room, listening to

- Credence Clearwater Revival, Aretha Franklin, the Rolling Stones.
- The house we had to leave when we moved to the Central Valley,
- the summer I began calling a different address home, instead of
- that easy string of numbers attached to some boy's name.

Slice of Your Life

- Sometimes referred to as "bricks and mortar," houses are much more than the physical materials from which they're built. Especially when it's *your* house and *your* feelings in *those* rooms. Take a tally of the houses you've lived in or spent a significant amount of time in—homes of grandparents, cousins, and friends *all* count. Write out each string of house numbers and the names of the corresponding streets, avenues, roads, cul-de-sacs, ways. Describe one house on the outside, and include a few memories that happened on the inside, too. Begin with *Here's the house . . .*
- Places, like certain people, can leave invisible marks on us. Name a few places (or people) that have left their marks on *you*. Hint: it's probably a place you either wish you could return to or never want to step foot in again. Somewhere in your writing, mention a type of weather (sunshiny, sticky, cloudy with a chance of rain), an appliance, a hiding place, a made-up color (see page 73).
- Imagine your footprint somewhere on earth. Describe the exact spot on the planet where its indentation exists. Use this as the beginning of a longer story. Quick, the wind's picking up, better make it a haibun or haiku (see page 81).

Your Turn

On-the-Spot Drop

SECRET HIDING PLACES

Look within! The secret is inside you.

—*Hui-neng*

Hiding when you're older is fun. (Really. I still do it.) Find a secret spot where you can slip from view. A place *nobody* knows about, except maybe a close friend or a dog who won't bark at you.

Before entering, imagine you're going on a long car trip. With a wide-leg stance, interlace your fingers behind your back and fold forward, extending your arms straight up in the air. (Bent like this, you might feel like an ostrich.) Then stand back up and place your palms on your shoulders. With the points of your elbows, spell out some secret words or initials in the air. When ready, disappear from view.

Once in your hiding place, you can say things—secret things—to a piece of paper that you can't always speak to the light of day or the star-dark of night. Skip this page if you don't like secrets. Stay if you do. By the way, this kind of secret telling doesn't have *anything* to do with betraying a trust. It's about truth telling, in *whatever* form *you choose*. I can't remember who said

94

it, but here's a piece of advice I keep close: *If you've lived it, seen it, or felt it, it's your story, too. You have a right to tell your story any way you choose.*

Drop Deeper

- Write "I could not—or I can't—tell" and begin your list. Lay down a few fake secrets first, then dig in and see how many electric real-life secrets you can reveal. Write until you feel your true power spark.
- Pretend every part of your body has a secret language. Discover what your hands would say you've done, your feet, your knees, your mouth, your teeth. Find out *which* part of your body knows *what*. (My knees know to stay off soccer fields, my head knows to trust my heart, my eyebrows know how to hang out above it all.)
- What do you want to run from? What do you run toward?
- Offer advice to someone who skipped this page but may return later. Allow six words or fewer per line, and share a few places where *your* poems hide out.

I'll Tell You a Secret

Poems hide. Just like people.
Look around, wherever you are—
Don't be shy. You're alive.
Ask yourself what you most need
to find. Look up, straight
into your own patch of sky.
Breathe in the lake, count
the bees where they hover
above blossoming trees.
In the middle of the night,

rise from your bed,
walk through the quiet
of each painted room.
Outside, rest your palms
on the moist ground.
Invite in the clouds,
the slivered moon.
Listen to your heartbeat.
Are you brave enough?
Of course, you are.
Now pick up a pen
and write it all down.

—Katrina Trelawny

Your Turn

SAY CHEESE

We're posed on a wooden bridge in Alum Rock Park. Mom's wearing oval glasses. Dad's beard is too long. My smile, trying too hard as my sister stands barefoot, refusing to give in to the camera. This much I know is true: I want this photo to prove that we're a happy family. So I curl my fingers around my sister's neck to get her to hold still and face the right way. Refusing, she whines that she wants to go home and to ride her new bike minus training wheels. Our parents can't see that our lives are melting under a cloudless sky. A stranger in a cowboy hat shouts *Say cheese*. The black box focuses; the shutter clicks closed.

On the drive home, I pout in the backseat while my mother coaxes, "Oh, never mind who wasn't looking forward, holding still, Katrina." (Katrina, her nickname for me.)

In front of the garage, Dad sets up the ramp he built out of two-by-fours and old plywood. My sister asks me to ride with her, but I refuse. Instead I sit on the porch and listen to my father call out *Beautiful,* and clap for her instead. She's receiving all the attention I refuse. My mother opens the screen door and reminds me it's a choice I'm making, letting her ride that red bike for both of us. I only shrug and pretend I couldn't care less. I close my eyes when my sister skids and calls out my name, as if I'm the one who had nearly died.

Later, I challenge her to a race from the garage up to the living room. I win, turn a cartwheel, then stand victorious on the leather chair Mom bought at a yard sale. I convince my sister this chair is the *only* boat that will save us. Pretending to set sail, I hang over the edge and lower the rope of my voice.

Alligators, I wave. *They're swimming to get you.*

Nooooo, she cries. *Wait for me!*

I pretend to be a tourist, with a camera. *Smile,* I say, using my pointer fingers to snap a shot. Each time she scrambles for safety onto my boat, I push her off.

Alligators, I warn. *They're going to eat you.* I aim and click my make-believe camera.

Mom! she cries, complaining I'm teasing, taking her picture like that.

Smile, I whisper. (Click. Click. Click.)

She pulls her arms inside her T-shirt and holds her breath. Her cheeks, rosy and wet. Dust motes and tension flood the room. In the end, I am the one in the picture, balanced on the bow of a sinking boat.

Slice of Your Life

- Write about a time you did something and someone cried.
- Write about a time someone did something and *you* cried.
- What have you been teased about? Whom have you teased?
- What snapshot moments have you memorized?

Your Turn

GIVEAWAY PARTY

To get the full value of joy you must have someone
to divide it with.

—Mark Twain

I t's been said that the world is run on two economies: a money economy, where the most important thing is counting and keeping track, and a gift economy, where the most important thing is keeping something for a while and then passing it on. Which economy do you live in? Which economy would you *like* to live in? Hint: you know you're living in a gift economy when you're not concerned about making everything "even-steven."

Finish some of the sentence-starters on the next page, then multiply your answers until you have two of everything (or maybe more), and throw a party, giving away a few lines in the form of a poem. Jessica gave away the small road on the right and that distant god in her soul; Madeline, the footsteps of a bear and her lucky hand that she writes with. Alexis gave away her voice as a token of love and trust. Start your poem with "I give you." The "you" can be anyone and everyone. It's OK to answer with the literal kind of truth *and* the stretchy-bendy kind of truth. (You already investigated what stretches on page 3.)

A combination of senses that I like (mix sight, smell, taste, touch, sound words) is:

- warm fur and wild mint, wet sand and a symphony of crickets, butterscotch and the heat of a bonfire, light from a full moon mixed with the distant call of loons above the crash of salty waves.

My ultimate birthday meal (including dessert) is:

_____

My favorite coin and the side (heads or tails) I most often call:

_____

Something small you'd find in my closet or backpack:

_____

A place I feel safe:

_____

A sound from nature that calms me:

_____

My favorite letters and corresponding colors:

_____

My most prized possession:

_____

Here's a recipe for (pick an emotion):

_____

Here's an echo of (pick anything except a sound):

_____

Three things I'd want if stranded on a desert island:

_____

Herc's the view from my bedroom window:

_____

An article of clothing I wish I'd never outgrow:

_____

A piece of sporting equipment I regularly use:

_____

My favorite place to play as a child:

_____

The footsteps of (pick a wild animal):

_____

A friend I like to hang out with:

_____

My favorite breakfast cereal:

_____

The Monopoly token I reach for first is:

_____

The day and month I was born:

_____

My favorite playing card in the deck:

_____

FOUND POEMS

Found poems are like the world's secret treasure chest that *everyone* has access to. All you need is the code. Get ready, grab a pen—I'm about to give it to you. But you have to swear you'll pass it on.

OK, so all you need to find found-poem treasure is to copy down words, phrases, fragments, and entire sentences *exactly* as you see them written or hear them spoken. And guess what? They're *everywhere:* hiding in plain sight. On ordinary road signs. The covers of magazines. In book titles, chapter headings, and newspaper articles. Written on candy wrappers. Scribbled on notes passed during class. On jars of jam, bottles of shampoo. Found-poem treasure can be had for the taking in any library, school cafeteria, classroom, convenience store, shopping mall, park, or basketball court *near you.* Off that poster hanging on the wall above your bed, across a billboard, down a dark alley, and on that wall of graffiti.

Many poets incorporate snippets of found-poem texts into their own verses. *The Waste Land* by T. S. Eliot includes parts of an opera, Greek mythology, and lines from Shakespeare. Found-poem treasure can be made into lines that you fit together and arrange into minimum length for maximum strength for any silly, serious, or silerious search for poem-pleasure. If this sounds *way* too easy, it is.

Here's a found poem made from three road signs + a quote taped to my computer screen + a note on a seventh-grade classroom door + the front of a greeting card.

Blind Curves Ahead

Slow to 10 m.p.h.
Start seeing everything as god
but keep it a secret.
Merge, proceed with caution.
This is a quiet zone. Poet at work.
Bullying and put-downs not allowed.
Caution: guard cat on duty.

EVERYWHERELOOK

In Oxford, England, Katrina Trelawny locks the door of her flat at 23 Observatory Street and walks toward the Woodstock Road Deli. On her way, she passes a woman with an angel-smile, riding a bicycle with a wicker basket on the handlebars. She passes a man with a white mustache who, like a true gentleman, offers her the sidewalk's narrow right-of-way. At the corner, she nods to a construction worker whose job it is to wear a yellow vest and stand at a gate with a sign that reads: KINDLY SLOW DOWN. She steps around a group of students clomped together talking and notices the trash collector, wheeling a rubbish bin toward the back of his truck. As he flips a switch that opens the compactor's jaws, a wish surfaces inside Katrina that he, too, could still be in school. A bus whizzes past and lifts the edge of her polka-dot skirt just as she steps through the front door of her favorite lunch spot. Greeted by the woman with short-cropped hair and a nose ring, every table taken except for one, Katrina claims it by setting her sweater across the back of a chair. At the counter, she orders a cup of squash soup and a rocket salad. "Do you want seeds on that?" the woman with the nose ring asks. "Yes, please," Katrina answers in her best British, before ordering the last slice of chocolate pie. She watches a couple near the window steal a kiss then carries her lunch back to her table. Settling in, she notices the poster above her announcing an exhibition of poodle portraits at the Jam Factory, silver against blue, the words all run together: E V E R Y W H E R E L O O K. She takes a sip of soup and smiles her own angel smile, since *that's* what she loves to do.

Story Starters

- Every*where*look. Be alive to *all* the miniature worlds happening around you, *all* the time. Start with a route you walk every day, mention a common courtesy, include a stray snatch of dialogue: "Do you want seeds with that?" Describe something whizzing past, something in the sky, something that makes you want to laugh, wonder why, look away.
- It's been said that for those who wonder, wonders appear. Create a favorite character or alter ego (Katrina Trelawny is mine) and take an inventory of everything she/he wonders about in the course of an afternoon.
- Make up your horoscope (or horror-scope) today. Perhaps begin by reading yours in the newspaper and elaborate on it—take it in a new direction, argue with it, or defend it.

Your Turn

NEAT FREAKS
AND MUD PIES

So what if I want the cereal boxes organized by height, if I sort and arrange my socks by color? I crave order. I like my peanut-butter-and-honey sandwiches cut diagonally. I want the crusts left off my bread. I make lists, my bed, beg my sister to let me tame her snarls into ponytails so I can show her off to my friends. I'm prissy, but in a good way—sensitive, imaginative, occasionally argumentative. My parents are hippies who shop secondhand stores, our living room an odd mix of flea-market chic—wind chimes, driftwood, bold-patterned pillows. My father, the Buddhist-builder, attempts his own brand of reasoning with me, explaining that the grass in the backyard is *always* going to grow . . . so why must I insist on fighting the weeds back down? He encourages me to accept each dandelion, calling them *beautiful* like my straw-colored hair. Of course, he has no clue that I'm staking the happiness of my childhood on the appearance of our yard, that I want a new life, and a new name to go with it. So while my sister makes mud pies by the falling-down fence and crushes up pebbles for frosting, I run to find the manual mower inside the cobwebby shed. I imagine my father whistling, *Looks pretty good, Sweetheart*, when I finish. Lost in daydream, I push the dull blades in straight green lines, my own screams jolting me out of my reverie. By the plum tree,

Mom slaps the mound of mud over my swollen foot where the stinger has poked its way in. On uneven grass, my sister and I sit, our eyes dazed with tears, listening to explanations about bare feet and bumblebees and why Mom had to go and ruin that pie. Why *everything* grows, gets messy, evolves, and eventually must die. (Sigh.)

Slice of Your Life

- What kind of kid are/were you? Include how you like your sandwiches served.
- Leap off the line: OK, here's what (who) I'd change.
- How did you get that scrape, bruise, sting, scar?
- Describe how to make a mud pie. What? You've *never* made a mud pie? Drop this book *immediately* and go find some dirt. Turn on the hose. Come back later and write. (Maybe wash your hands first.)

Your Turn

Surprise Yourself Survey

YOUR TRUE NAME

Your true name has the secret power to call you.

—Vera Nazarian

Your true name isn't always the name you were given at birth, especially since you had absolutely *no choice* in the matter. Sometimes your true name lives *beneath* your earth suit and looks back at you in the mirror. Finding your true name can hold the power to help you remember who you *really* are. Here are some suggestions on fooling around with words and images to locate it.

My friend Laurel was digging in her garden one afternoon when she found her true name: *Wild-Frizzy-Haired-Woman-Who-Loves-Lettuces*. I've heard kids your age let loose and rename themselves: *Somersault-Sparrow-Who-Flies-Her-Own-Way-Home; Turn-Around-Jump-Shot-Shooter; Sprinter-Across-a-Sunny-Field-Ablaze-with-Bees*. Even older, taller kids discover their true names, sometimes on an NBA basketball court, like *Metta World Peace*.

If you're having a hard time loosening up enough to find your true name, hang out with a second grader and borrow some silliness, start a pillow fight, or choose a one-word nature name like the counselors at my son's favorite sleepaway camp: Bobcat, Osprey, Starfish, Fox. (On the drive home, I named myself Moonbeam, another mom claimed Wildflower.) Ask yourself what nature name is *yours*. Pull on a spirit of adventure. Pick up a pen. Pile on word after word to the beginning lines below. Play with options. Write fast or slow. Say *no sirree* to making too much sense.

My name really means

dreamer who whispers to all that waits beneath the trapdoor of her heart, sure-footed acrobat queen, brave warrior who paints the outline of a mountain around her shiny life.

⋮

Here's the story behind the name I was given _____

_____

I was almost named _____

Nicknames I like _____

Today my name means too many _____

Yesterday it meant too little _____

Tomorrow my name might turn into _____

It's the wish of _____

Inside my name is hidden _____

When my mom calls my name, I feel _____

_____

Secretly I know my name is _____

My name was born when _____

My name travels toward _____

Between the letters of my name hides _____

_____

Consider exploring further:

What does your name hold the scent of?

_____

What does your name have the softness of?

_____

Where would you look if you lost your name?

_____

RESPONSIBILITY AND A BRIDGE TO THE MOON

Another campground. This one in Kentucky. Late June, my sister and I finish our dinner—spaghetti with tofu and garlic bread—while Mom boils water to wash the dishes and Dad pulls a flashlight from his backpack. Placing it in my hand, he asks if I'll take my sister to brush her teeth before bed. In charge yet again, I rev up a low-level grumble, then remember the lake I spotted earlier that I wanted to swim across. What better place to brush our teeth? *Sure, I'll take her*, I say. Of course, I don't mention the lake. I know my father meant for us to hike the well-lit path to the camp bathroom and hike straight back. As soon as we're far enough down the path, I use my magic powers to entice my sister to kick rocks down the black road, promising she can hold the magic flashlight. The wind races through us, parting the trees' needled boughs. Far from Gordon Avenue, we cut across a field of cattails, stopping to make certain it's only the cicadas hissing their songs. The night races out fast in all directions, surrounding us, pulling us toward some invisible vortex that's stronger than my ten-year-old magic powers. And when my sister whines that she's afraid the dark is walking too close behind us, I point at the moon and promise to build her a bridge to touch the stars. Together we make a thin trail to the lake. It's here I pull her into my story, not knowing it will take something stronger than a love of deep water and the magic of a promise to hold us together.

Slice of Your Life

- Write about a time you had to act braver than you felt. Where were you? Who were you with? No need to write the ending yet.
- Pick a month, time of day, or heavenly body—the moon, a star, Venus—and use it for a title. Then write a letter to your "good angel," who knows and loves you no matter what you have or haven't done. Tell him/her what you want to accomplish, what you need for protection.
- Pinpoint a spot on earth when you felt bold and daring. What risk—real or imagined—was involved? What magic?
- Describe the feeling of diving headfirst or swimming in the deep end (of anything).

Your Turn

WAYS OF WATCHING

You can observe a lot just by watching.

—*Yogi Berra*

Sitting in stillness can help us to see everyday things—even ourselves—from a different vantage point, and feel the appreciation we have for our friends, family, pets, the world, the moon, our expanding life views. One morning in a hotel room, my son woke up in the rumpled bed next to where I was meditating and insisted that the glass nightstand was an iceberg. I looked at it through his just-waking-up eyes, and it was, most definitely, an iceberg.

To explore a different way of watching, it helps to find a quiet place all your own: on the last step, under a tree, against a friend's back, if you ask and they're willing. Sit cross-legged or with legs stretched out straight, and lift up out of your waist. Feel the length of your spine. Roll your neck in *s-l-o-w* clockwise circles. Let whatever's crammed in your mind *unwind* counterclockwise. Notice if you start to wonder if there's a text to check or someone else's back to lean against. Notice how the enjoyment of your breath can be gentle, like petting the ears of a rabbit. Feel the places where your clothing touches your skin. Be aware of your sit bones—a.k.a. rump, bottom, derriere, booty—in contact with the ground.

Keep noticing what you notice—the tug of the wind, the crows' cawing conversations, the boy across the creek calling for his dog, *Lou-ie!* Then choose *one thing* from your awareness field. It might arrive in the form of your nightstand, your left hand, possibly even a turtle, like it did for Fernando. Observe this *one* thing in five ways. Leave your observations as they are, or arrange them into a five-part poem or story.

Drop Deeper

- The poet Wallace Stevens wrote a famous poem, "Thirteen Ways of Looking at a Blackbird." Come up with five ways or situations of looking at *one* thing. Here are five ways that Mr. Stevens saw the same bird. (Find the eight ways that are missing.)

From *Thirteen Ways of Looking at a Blackbird*

I
Among twenty snowy mountains,
The only moving thing
Was the eye of the blackbird.

II
I was of three minds,
Like a tree
In which there are three blackbirds.

III
The blackbird whirled in the autumn winds.
It was a small part of the pantomime.

IX
When the blackbird flew out of sight,
It marked the edge
Of one of many circles.

XII
The river is moving.
The blackbird must be flying.

—Wallace Stevens

Five Turtle Observations

1
All I ever wanted was a turtle.

2
OK, so the truth is turtles walk slow.

3
Maybe if we could walk faster
no one would make fun of us.

4
I wonder what it would be like
to live inside a turtle's shell.

5
Does it ever seem like you're always lonely?

—Fernando

Your Turn

FILL HALF A PAGE WITH Y-O-U

The truth of a thing is the feel of it, not the think of it.

—Stanley Kubrick

Along the journey of your creative life, when you write— and even when you're not writing—allowing yourself to be surprised is of *supreme* importance. So much possibility lives in the realm of your willingness not to know everything in advance but to feel what's happening in the surprise of right-now instead. Take a secret mission adventure with this survey and discover—via *feeling* rather than thinking. Answer in the spirit of riding *off-road*, where there are twists and turns, and you get to discover the you that is "you-er than you," to quote Dr. Seuss. Luckily you can't do this being you thing wrong.

Be willing *not* to know. Play around and experiment with creating something that lets you find the you that's "truer than true." What have you got to lose?

To cool my anxiety, I imagine

the moon as my companion, a soft crunch of risk and loose bits of
found time coating the outside of each cloud, firefly, pebble, as I
venture through a curtain of fog, into the tree-lined distance.

•
•
•
•
•

Every part of me has a secret language. My hands reach for

_____

My feet run toward _____

My neck aches for _____

My eyes search across _____

My soul wonders if _____ _____

My heart insists on _____

To cool my anxiety, I imagine _____

Here are a few images I can juggle: _____

Here's what I trapeze between: _____

If you open the trapdoor of my heart, you'll find _____

_____

Pick three answers from your survey and link them any way you choose into a poem that doesn't have to make sense. The only requirement: to utterly and completely surprise yourself right here, right now. Maybe you'll even whisper a little *Wow*. (See page 225 on *Yes, No,* and *Wow* possibilities.)

_____

_____

_____

_____

LIVING IN NOW

There's Collin. He's not living in the groundless future or in the already-lived past. But square-in-the-center of *NOW*'s shiny timelessness. Right here, where life feels reckless and true. Where all the cracks show and it's OK *not* to know what to do. Shadows dance beneath his size 8 feet. He shrugs when told his laces don't match—one green, one blue. He pedals off on a new trail up the mountain, never mind packing a map. This being instead of doing, living instead of performing, tastes like a double scoop of freedom with a dollop of whipped ease. He finds comfort in living just as he pleases. Along the way, he watches ants march their small step formation, counts clouds dancing their lazy spirals. Living in *now* instead of *not yet* can be dangerously fun, though it takes practice to remain in the realm of all that's unknown. *Now* instead of *later,* when C. might own that longed-for tennis racquet or snazzy pair of high-top shoes. He smiles his winning smile, feels deep in his lengthening bones that he knows life's not a race up a long flight of stairs, but a gentle allowing his heart to stay open, so he can belt out whatever song comes rumbling along.

Story Starters

- Arthur Miller, a famous American playwright and essayist, said, "The word *now* is like a bomb thrown through the window, and it ticks." Describe the room you're in right now with as much color, clarity, and detail as you dare. Include *everything* that holds right-now light, interest, intensity, rhythm for you (the color of your shoelaces, your mom reminding you to pack a map, fill your water bottle). Go with where your writing wants to wander.
- Be curious about your own daydreaming. What's the picture hiding behind your eyes? The song inside your ears, heart, throat? The truest right-now message being sent and felt? Tune in. Put an X-ray gaze on the *inside*. Take a snapshot with your pen. Quick, catch it. Everything's about to change.

Your Turn

GESTURES THAT SPEAK

I was the queen of giving a certain look or nonverbal clue to let you know *exactly* what was on my mind, a warning that I was about to fold up my Monopoly board and go home. Fearing my own voice—I know, crazy, right?—I would show my annoyance with a suggested sigh or roll of my eyes, to show what I felt *minus* any words. I was a pouter, a sulker, a moper, a brooder. With a raised eyebrow and a jut of my chin, I could shoot daggers from my eyes and had perfected the silent treatment. My cousin Dawnie would beg me (on her hands and knees) to say something, *p-l-e-a-s-e*. She'd apologize for things she hadn't done, promise to never do x, y, or z ever again, if only I would talk to her. I was, in a word, mean (to her and to myself, as not talking hurts the mute one the most). Gestures and looks were all I thought I had to protect myself. Silence was my shield.

What gestures do you use to show how you feel? How do you protect yourself without using words? Add some preferred gestures to the list on the next page, then decide what a few might mean to you or to a character in a story. Then play translator and put words, explanations, descriptions to those select gestures.

Update: I no longer use the silent treatment, and do attempt—

though still a challenge with certain people—to say what I mean and mean what I say.

A pat on the head	A hand through hair	A backing away
A wink and a nudge	A tilt of the head	A purse of the lips
A roll of the eyes	A clench of the fist	A pucker of the lips
A pout of the lips	A stomp of the foot	The baring of teeth
A shrug of the shoulders	A fake smile	The knit of a brow
A scrunch of the nose	A looking away	The gazing away

Add two of the above together and write what happens next. . . .

OPENERS AND STARTERS

It was impossible to get a conversation going, everybody was talking too much.

—Yogi Berra

Here are the beginnings of conversation-starter poems to use on or off the page. Write until you're ready for another opener to carry you to a different place in the labyrinth of your imagination's verbal passageways. Back and forth, like a tennis match, or a conversation you might have with yourself, a sibling, a close friend, or a cat who knows how to listen between the pause (without using his claws). Write a dialogue between you and that friend who knows how to listen *and* tell a good story, who likes you just as you are, totally *gets* you, thinks you're hilarious, understands you even when you aren't making sense. That friend.

The only thing missing is

those nights after swim practice, cuddled up with bowls of noodle soup . . . Mom reminding us to finish our dinner, Dad making us dessert. That look, travelling between us, that said without saying, *We scored.*

I keep wondering if _____

But what I really want to know is _____

Do you remember when _____

All I ever wanted was _____

OK, the truth is _____

I wonder what it would be like to _____

If only there was _____

Maybe if we could _____

When I least expect it, sometimes I _____

It's like the world has changed into _____

Wouldn't it be fun if we could _____

Hey, I have an idea, let's _____

I was just wondering if _____

OVERHEARD CONVERSATIONS

Everything in the world has a spirit released by its sound.

—*John Cage*

All writers do it, especially when first figuring out *how* to write it. Dialogue, that is. We listen. We overhear. OK, let's call it what it is—we *eavesdrop*. We have to. But we don't do it to spread gossip or to create a smear campaign about people who shall remain nameless. At least, that's not what *this* overheard experiment is encouraging.

All I'm suggesting is that you get out of the house, the classroom, your typical checking-who-just-sent-a-text routine. Take in a change of scenery. Put yourself in close proximity to people, hunker down, and *really* listen. Catch every word, every pause, each language-beat. Your aim: to capture and learn how to imitate on the page exactly how people communicate or *don't* communicate. We all have different paces, filler words, interruption methods, listening modes . . . Some speak in complete sentences, others leave words out. Some answer in one-word responses or attach a questioning upward lilt to whatever they say. Really? (Yes, really.) Some tend to use more than their fair share of "like" and "you know." (Like, you know the ones.)

Your job: get close, stay out of the way, quiet down, be discreet. Go to a café, sit on a park bench, hide in the passenger seat (with the windows rolled down). Then just listen. That's all. Gather up what you hear and jot it down any way you can. Here's a one-way conversation I overheard near a middle school a few miles north of where I live. I wrote it on a popsicle wrapper—the only paper I had. (Note to self: remember your notebook!)

- Listen, Honey, I talked to Aunt Ella.
- Hysterical. Uh-huh.
- Yelling at Aunt Irene again.
- That's right . . .
- Well, it's looking better than it did, but we have to prepare
    ourselves.
- She's not a young woman anymore.
- Well, yes, there is that. Uh-huh, uh-huh.
- And all the money she owes.
- The prosecutor said she made some poor choices.
- Two years minimum.
- Honey, we all know Aunt Ella can be a handful.

Drop Deeper

- Make up a story about Aunt Ella. What did she do? Why did she yell at Aunt Irene? What did the person on the other cell phone say in response? Imagine who Honey is.
- Listen to a conversation, record it on the page *exactly* as you hear it, then go back later—days, weeks, months later—read it out loud, and edit it *waaay* down. Give the conversation a major haircut.
- Write a poem made entirely of words you overhear today.

Your Turn

On-the-Spot Drop

THE SOUND OF IT

I love deadlines. I like the whooshing sound they make
as they fly by.

—Douglas Adams

I just learned the word *noise* comes from the Latin word for sickness, which is *nausea*. So that explains it: too much noise and I feel agitated and confused. Too long spent in silence and I grow thirsty for conversation. (Too many deadlines and I go a little cuckoo crazy.) How about you? What's your sound-to-silence threshold? What do you like that *whooshes* by? Writers tend to need more silence than most. But, come on, a steady diet of *anything* can get bor-ing.

Give this a whirl: bask in a room of silence, then turn up the volume of a favorite song. Grab a few words from the air and forget about their meaning as you say them over and over and over. After a while, do you even recognize what you're saying? How do certain words make you feel? Say a few out loud, turn them around in your mouth. Let their sound loosen and expand. Long before images and mind pictures, long before meaning and sense—long before deadlines—there is *pure sound* . . . and your feelings. Music is inspirational to many writers because it evokes feeling. (Maybe this is why many of us go on dates to concerts.)

Find those words that make *your* mouth feel like you're savoring a slice of fruit pie. Write "Say," and pile on a few mouthwatering word-bites. Taste each one. Here's part of a poem by Marilyn Krysl called "Saying Things" that gives my ears and mouth a surprise party when I say it out loud:

Say bellows, say sledge,
say threshold, cottonmouth, Russian leather,
say ash, picot, fallow deer, saxophone, say kitchen sink.

Drop Deeper

- Hunt for overheard tasty bits of conversation. "Oh, my Maggie's a wicked pickle!" (Snatched up by my ears while in a London pharmacy last summer.) Find sounds from right where you are: that *squeaky-scuff* off the bottom of your sneakers, the *thwappy* sound of air rushing through an open window.
- Gather words that rhyme or nearly rhyme—this is a *slant rhyme*. How many can you find? How many can you string together? Warning: this won't and need not make sense.

Lassitude . . . solitude
Teenage . . . renegade . . . lemonade
Ice cream . . . long dream.
Distance . . . existence
Lipstick . . . music
Check, text . . . mixed-up.
(Keep going!)

- Find a few words that you love. Combine, play, trade, rearrange them *within* your writing. What you write doesn't have to look like a poem.

I'll trade a slice of my lassitude for a piece of your solitude, your
teenage renegade for a cold lemonade, an ice cream cone for a
soft-serve summer dream, my red car if you'll walk this far into
the distance of our existence; a fast dance to rock music for a kiss
without lipstick; one text from you and I'm all mixed-up.

Shark's Teeth

Everything contains some
silence. Noise gets
its zest from the
small shark's-tooth-
shaped fragments
of rest angled
in it. An hour
of city holds maybe
a minute of these
remnants of a time
when silence reigned,
compact and dangerous
as a shark. Sometimes
a bit of tail
or fin can still
be sensed in parks.

—Kay Ryan

Your Turn

SNATCHED FROM THE RADIO

Radio is the theater of the mind.

—Steve Allen

Flip on the radio. Catch a few word-bites from the news, off a traffic report, in the middle of an annoying ad, from the lyrics of a favorite song. Then, just as quickly, turn the volume dial down and add the snippet you just heard to the list below. Tip: this snatching-up words and phrases game doesn't work as well with television, since the visuals get in the way.

Use what you catch for leap-off prompts to get warmed-up for your next round of writing. Listen with a friend. Decide in advance to catch only a set number of syllables if you like, then create a poem using syllabic verse. (Turn to page 228 for a description of syllabics.)

They'll be back a little later . . .

It's still slow, stretching out beyond . . .

Ninety seconds before the hour and . . .

What we need for California's future is . . .

If you take a peek at a map, you'll see . . .

She switched the lights back on to find . . .

Here's a key that opens a door to . . .

Keep going, along the silk road of . . .

These are the warnings you must forget . . .

Like skeletons on fire we . . .

Nine hundred years later . . .

Here's the mask I like to wear . . .

Oh, that's very difficult to do . . .

This doesn't have to be your destiny . . .

Both things can exist . . .

Without humor I can't . . .

Sitting on top of the world with my legs hanging free . . .

Here's a new band from Iceland . . .

DIALOGUE TAGS AND ACTION BEATS

With dialogue, you already know you want to make sure it sounds like regular speech. No lectures. No long-winded explanations. Of course in real life, some people do go on and on. And on. We all know a few. But dialogue, good dialogue anyway, *has* to cut to the chase. So aim for *brevity*.

Good dialogue *shows* what a character in your story is thinking *and* feeling. Good dialogue can be funny, sad, or scary, all depending on the tag. "Wait, what's a tag?" you ask. The tag's the *he said, she said, you ask* part of the sentence. Unlike the purists, I say go ahead and use other dialogue tags, too, especially since we all whisper, shout, scream, agree, mumble, demand, deny, laugh, and cry in addition to *ask*.

Whatever you do, though, *don't* fall into the telling trap, when you ought to be doing the work of *showing*. That's where action beats come in. "Whoa, slow down," you say with eyebrows raised. "What's an action beat?" The action beat is when you *show* the action (for example, *with eyebrows raised*). Notice I didn't say *tell* the action, by using an adverb. (Avoid adverbs the way you avoid false friends.) You wouldn't use the action beat to say, "Well, I don't know about that," she said suspiciously. Instead you'd use the action beat to *show* what this suspicious person looks like. "Well, I don't know about that," she said with raised eyebrows. Can you see and feel how the subtle raising of those eyebrows *shows* the suspicion?

Here are some other action tags:

"Oh, yeah?" he winked.

"Oh, yeah?" her mouth tightened.

"Oh, yeah?" his eyes narrowed.

"Oh, yeah?" she smirked.

"Oh, yeah?" he looked away.

Hint

· See how the above "Oh, yeahs" mean very different things, depending on the action tag used? What other action or dialogue tags could be used after *Oh, yeah?* Ditto: *No way. How cool is that? Right now?* (Right now.)

PATIENCE AND TEETH

My teeth are as crooked and spaced apart as a wild jack-o'-lantern. My right front tooth is bucked, chipped, and turning yellow. I have an underbite and a cross bite. There's a lot going on in there. Dr. Hausrath uses cutting-edge methods to close gaps and straighten misaligned chompers. The wires are sharp and cut my gums. The torture starts near the end of middle school. Shy, with a mouth full of metal, this is the summer my family will move from the Bay Area to a small town at the top of the Central Valley. We have visited Red Bluff exactly once, and now we're moving there. What *are* my parents thinking?! Mom says she likes the idea of a small town, Dad the lower cost of living. They assure me I'll love my new school where the classes are small and the nuns wear Birkenstock sandals. With a wad of wax stuffed between my cheek and gums, I say my good-byes to Kristin, Paisley, Betsy—wave to Mike—then climb into the backseat of our white VW van beside my sister, and watch Gordon Avenue recede from view.

The new orthodontist takes one look at my "modern" braces and informs my mother they *have* to be removed. Yes, all of them. He uses a different kind of orthodonture. He uses the word *orthodonture*. Temperatures soar to triple digits. Trapped in a reclined position in an air-conditioned office above the Sacramento River, I count ceiling tiles stained the same color as my tooth and listen to a loop of James Taylor songs piped through dusty speakers while thirty-two bands and wires are removed, reattached, and retightened onto the thirty-two bones of my teeth. Reminding myself to breathe, I don't flinch. Instead I imagine the heat waves outside shimmering into peace signs, the kids inner-tubing down the river, inviting me along, my parents and sister up the road in our rental house on Sherman Drive, unpacking boxes in the new living room. With my head tipped back, eyes closed under bright lights, mouth held open, I know we aren't returning to the Bay Area anytime soon. As James Taylor croons for the umpteenth time "You've Got a Friend," I focus on the smile I might acquire by the end of high school, willing myself to stay calm, cool, relaxed, true.

Slice of Your Life

- What about teeth, your teeth, your best friend's teeth, your cat's missing tooth, the cage of your braces, your dog's overbite? Find out *how much* or how little you have to say on the topic of dental details. If your writing leads into other territory—your family taking a trip or moving, the trauma (drama) of starting a new school, the heat waves of summer, or the patience required to be where you are rather than where you aren't—*go there.* Forget about teeth.
- Put on some music and write a profile of your dentist or orthodontist. Include what his breath smells like and decide if you get annoyed when he asks you questions while his hands are in your mouth.
- If you could live anywhere, where would this anywhere place be? Include your deepest wish for yourself.

Your Turn

THE STUFF OF US

If you have a skeleton in your closet, take it out
and dance with it.

—Carolyn Mackenzie

Open your closet. Pull out the drawers of your desk. Empty your backpack, gym bag, pockets, wallet, purse. Sit for a while among all your *stuff*. Chances are you have *a lot* more *everything* than you ever touch, use, or know what to do with. (I know I do.) Books, clothes, shoes, CDs, stationery, sports equipment, games, jewelry, trophies, lotions, potions, *so many* assorted collections. Acquiring is something we in the developing world have gotten pretty good at. Maybe too good. Growing up, my best friend Kristin collected her toenail clippings. Yes, she did. My cousin Dawnie collected glass bells. One of my neighbors collects cars. A lot of moms collect their kids' teeth. My son collects NBA jerseys and coins from distant countries. I collect rocks, quotes, poems, and handwritten notes.

Make a list of what you intentionally collect: stamps, shells, rubber bands, sports cards. Make a second list of what you don't consciously collect but are starting to see a pattern of collection emerging. Sit in the center of your room and observe: T-shirts (what is inked on the front?); electronics (what does each do?); books (titles, subtitles?); stray food (empty soda cans, graham cracker crumbs). Let the list roll on. Interview family members, neighbors, friends on what they collect. Be a reporter, a spy. Peer in windows. Then find a chair—move the stack of books that's on it first—and begin to write.

Drop Deeper

- Catalog *all* objects in a particular space: your closet, gym bag, the backyard, that drawer where an invisible force causes small objects to gravitate. Then *become* what you see, like Cheryl Strayed did in her memoir *Wild* when she wrote, "I was a pebble. I was a leaf. I was the jagged branch of a tree. I was nothing to them and they were everything to me."
- Connect the dots. Mix a little bit of your stuff with someone else's stuff to create another collection: words arranged on a page that will turn into yet *another* collection—a poem—to rest beneath your understanding (and uncluttered) gaze.

For Papa it was about baseball cards and small bottles
of scotch, the kind businessmen buy on long flights,
Nana in her pink robe and curlers
waiting with the porch light on to welcome him home.
For my father, the builder, it was nature he collected,
odd-sized pieces of oak, gnarled branches dragged back
after camping trips, refashioned into a bench or table.
He collected rocks and borrowed shells from the sea
where my sister and I scattered his ashes into dark waves
that day I would have traded all my belongings
for a chance to say a last good-bye.

—Karen

Your Turn

MAN AGAINST CHAIN-LINK FENCE

The streets are cold. Four men crouch on the sidewalk, sharing a cup of coffee. Walking past, a woman crosses to the other side of Telegraph. She's looking for something old—a clock for the mantel, dishes like the blue ones her mother set the table with—but she keeps seeing them: those men with bare arms against the chain-link fence. *Choose something,* she thinks. Inside the narrow shop, she walks the aisles lined with lamp shades, shot glasses, antique tables and chairs, imagining the man without any teeth who'd smiled at her. She imagines how he must have owned these things, too. *Things, just things,* she tells herself, the way he told himself, after he walked out of his life, left behind his marriage and kids. Just gave it all up: clock, jacket, dishes, wife, job, country.

Story Starters

- Venture into the world nearby, and observe one person you can't look away from. Create their backstory. At first, go with wild hunches and guesses as to who this person is. Add real details you notice, too (the man without any teeth who smiled at you), and include one or more objects (dishes like the blue ones her mother set the table with). Fact: for every person on our planet (six billion and growing), there are multiple stories to go with each life. The good news: we'll *never* run out of stories to hear or write about.

- Be a reporter with your eyes and ears. Just the facts. No imagination allowed. Bear witness to the next three people you see. In one short sketch, describe each one. Nothing more. Keep yourself—and the almighty "I"—out of it. By carefully selecting a few details, the reader's imagination will supply the rest.

Your Turn

On-the-Spot Drop

QUATRAINS THROUGH YOUR POET'S EYE

The world is but a canvas to our imagination.

—Henry David Thoreau

To view what's around you *as if* for the first time, it can be necessary to wander away from your everyday life, to get lost *on purpose*, lose track of time, leave home for a while so you can return with fresh eyes and a refocused imagination. So put this book aside, slip off your watch, and take a little walk into the distance of your existence.

Last winter, a group of sixth and seventh graders walked to my house each Wednesday for an experimental writing group. One evening, I gave them the "assignment" to wander around and just look at things. I gave them permission to open doors, peer into closets, check out bookshelves and cupboards. You know, the kind of snooping you want to do in other people's houses but don't because it's "not polite." I invited them to consider *all* the things they could look at and write about through their poets' eyes, while paying fresh attention to the world within my house.

(The cleared *and* cluttered spaces.) The idea was to write four lines—or a quatrain—about *one* object they found from their invited snoop and describe it in an entirely different light.

Go on your own snoop or pick something from the list that follows. *Anything* you can reach out and touch is up for grabs. If you ever walk over to write at my house, I'll let you snoop around, too.

On the first line: write the name of your object.

On the second line: compare it with something or rename it in a way that makes sense *to you*.

On the third line: add a dash of detail about what you wrote on line two.

On the fourth line: reassure it, ask it a question, say what it's doing, or what it's *like*.

pencil	bench	storm
candle	moon	mirror
doorway	window	face
dog	book	clock
whisper	shadow	shoe
quarter	piano	sock
cat	stone	wind chime
thumb	toothpick	tennis racquet
key	guitar	soup spoon

Thumb

odd, friendless boy
raised by four aunts,
don't worry, you're not alone.

—Philip Dacey

Clock

hands reach out to pull me in,
a land with a face
and no eyes.

—Mike

Here's another quatrain suggestion: Tip a four-letter word on its side and see what spills out, like Rebecca did.

Time travels through the ages to when
I met you and we tried to
Master being together until the
Exit opened and you fell out.

—Rebecca

Your Turn

_____   _____

_____   _____

_____   _____

_____   _____

_____   _____

_____   _____

_____   _____

THE MUSE OF BOOK SPINES

Muses work all day long and then at night
get together and dance.

—Edgar Degas

A muse is the source of an artist's inspiration. The first muses—daughters of Zeus and Mnemosyne (memory)—were a group of sisters who were also goddesses of the arts. The nine muse sisters are named Calliope (for heroic or epic poetry); Clio (for history); Erato (for lyric or love poetry); Euterpe (for music); Melpomene (for tragedy); Polyhymnia (for sacred poetry and mime); Terpsichore (for dancing and choral song); Thalia (for comedy); and Urania (for astronomy).

This On-the-Spot Drop experiment borrows from the incredibly talented and inspiring artist and writer Keri Smith, one of *my* muses for imaginative inspiration. (There's only one reason I would suggest you put down the book you're holding, and that's if you sprint out to buy Keri's books: *Finish This Book; Mess: The Manual of Accidents and Mistakes; Wreck This Journal; How to Be an Explorer of the World: Portable Life Museum;* and others). The latter is where this idea came from. And before Keri's muse sent it to her, it arrived via Nina Katchadourian's muse. Turns out,

153

the muse network is vast, intricate, *and* generous. Whimsical ideas spring into open hearts and wild minds. Like yours, Nina's, Keri's, mine. Are you ready? OK, here it is.

Take this book, and wander through the aisles of your local library, collecting *any* and *all* titles, subtitles, stray lines that catch your eye and cause your heart to smile, bloom, sway, quiver. Cover an entire page, front and back, so you have plenty of titles to arrange into a room of mused-upon words.

Drop Deeper

* Return to your creative-writing cave (like a bat cave only with sharpened pencils and snacks), and find your top ten titles. It's OK to tweak titles and combine word fragments if this helps you feel at home inside your found poem. Do whatever it takes to make what you find sing. If you want a title, call it "Found Poem from Stray Lines" like Mackenzie did.

Found Poem from Stray Lines

They lower me with ropes onto rocks
Into the natural order of things
This includes the gliding eye
From the green of the earth
Which it magnifies for coolness
I'll trade a fountain pen for an outboard motor
Ask forgiveness at the end
Life's darker than circumstance
I feel happiness
I feel I'm not alone

—Mackenzie

Your Turn

_____

_____

_____

_____

_____

_____

_____

_____

_____

_____

_____

_____

_____

_____

_____

_____

CENTO

In Latin, *cento* (pronounced "sen-toh") means "patchwork." A true cento poem takes single lines from other people's poems and patches or stitches them together in a new way. Think of a cento sort of like a word quilt. Centos are a *great* way of recycling, and we can *all* do more of *that*. But don't take my word for it. Don't take anyone's word for it . . . find out for yourself. Use your own eyes, ears, nose, tongue, fingers in order to see, hear, smell, taste, feel your "one wild and precious life," as poet Mary Oliver calls it. This way, you'll know firsthand what you're truly interested in, enough to invest those rippling hours of time parked at your desk with your notebook and pen.

To piece together a cento, copy five or ten different lines from different stories or poems *exactly* as they're written, and arrange them *however* they move you. If you're inspired to keep writing, go for it. If you get stalled, grab another piece of word fabric (a.k.a. a line from another poem) and continue to stitch.

Hints

- Centos can be found in any book. I let specific lines *find me*. Sometimes I begin to dream up my own lines of poetry as I stitch together the lines of other people's poems, creating what I call a *cento hybrid*. Mackenzie found her crossed-out poem cento from a page of comics in the *San Francisco Chronicle* (see below).

• One poet-friend, needing a break from writing, decided she could not create another image, simile, metaphor, or cento, so took a black Sharpie and began randomly crossing out words from a page of text (then another page, and another) until she found she had created an *entire* book. The words she *didn't* cross out became her cento, also called a cross-out poem.

Comic Strip Cento

Do you believe in everything?
Ghosts, time travel, Atlantis?
Then Washington is dead wrong about you.
You're a well-rounded individual.
You're really opening.
But your texts must stop using
all the world's exclamation marks.
Don't let this rough exterior fool you.
Usually 89% of the time I'm right.
This sure is quite an operation.
We owe all our success to the editors.

—Mackenzie

Poem in Which Words Have Been Left Out
—"The Miranda Rights," established in 1966

You have the right to remain
anything you can and will be.

An attorney you cannot afford
will be provided for you.

You have silent will.
You can be against law.
You cannot afford one.

You remain silent. Anything you say
will be provided to you.

The right can and will be
against you. The right provided you.

Have anything you say be
right. Anything you say can be right.

Say you have the right attorney.
The right remain silent.

Be held. Court the one. Be provided.
You cannot be you.

—Charles Jensen

WORD TICKETS

I've known all my life that I could take a bunch of words and throw them up in the air and they would come down just right.

—Truman Capote

Do you ever chance upon words that offer you the *exact* inspiration you need at the *exact* moment you need them? When this happens to me, I thank my lucky stars while my heart does a twist-and-shout shimmy dance. I love hearing the way a bunch of words fly through the air and find my ears, waking up my imagination to make a poem. Sometimes, though, when chance is on vacation and the clouds cover up my lucky stars, I actively go in search of the words I need, by creating handmade, multicolored word tickets like my poet-pal Susan Wooldridge does.

If you want to make your own inspiration words, get your hands on a roll of ADMIT ONE tickets—the kind of tickets you're given when you enter a raffle or see a movie—a pair of scissors, and any old newspaper, magazine, or book you don't mind ripping up (a book that belongs to you—and you can't think of a soul to pass it on to). Then simply cut out any and all words, groups of words, and stray fragments that catch your eye, ear, heart, intuition, interest. Amass your confetti-like cutouts into a pile. Then tape the cut-out words and word-combos onto your tickets. (When I do this with groups, we call out our favorites.) Keep your word tickets in a box or bag. I use a blue velvet bag that arrived holding a bottle of bubble bath. Anytime your lucky stars need aligning, you can pull out a handful of magic. Drop a few tickets into a poem you're writing on the spot and just like that: *ba-zing-ga*. You'll see. You can also toss a handful up into the air, like Truman Capote did, see where they land, and find your poem from there. Every few months I give my word tickets away and make a new batch so I always have a fresh supply. FYI: the giving-away part is just as fun as the making them part.

Drop Deeper

* Use the following lines to riff off or use for a title: *Right Now . . . The Lost World . . . Poetry Is . . .*
* Write your poem using your tickets. Put line breaks in where you'd breathe space into the poems below.

Right now, the world, just as it is, spinning trust inside its own orbit. Like two alligators fighting the green swamp of their hearts. Lines made from word tickets. Gravity: what a challenge. Alert for things like glowing scorpions, a plume of smoke, loneliness out among long shadows. Death between a father and a son. A great big heart of need and loss. History on a piece of paper. The king of shadows breaking his promise.

—Nathan

Thousands of miles away, white butterflies glow in the dark as if they were webs of light lost in the fog, in the vast world of time, death, and fire—winds that expand broader than the horizon as if they were flames. As the east sky grays, some light remains. The full moon steals the bridge to death, a supernova explodes hurtling fire and rock through time and space. The memory pasture goes up in quick flames. The lost world broadens in the horizon.

—Nicki

Your Turn

_____

_____

_____

_____

_____

_____

_____

_____

_____

_____

_____

_____

_____

PANTOUM

The *pantoum* arrived on the scene in the fifteenth century from Malaysian literature and was originally a kind of folk poem that was sung. Western writers altered the form into four-line stanzas—also called quatrains (see page 150)—which get repeated in a pattern, so that by the end of the poem *every line* is repeated, leaving the poem "filled with echoes." Pantoums are *great* containers for anything that you obsess over—your looks, a test, a swirly feeling caused by the attention from a certain girl or boy; *anything* you play and replay in your mind, hope to outrun and not get caught by (again).

The pattern to a pantoum is math-like. Lines 2 and 4 of each stanza are repeated as lines 1 and 3 of the next stanza, and so on. When I write pantoums, I keep the pattern in the margin, like a crib sheet. You can vary your repeated lines by tweaking certain words or the word order. And—here's where it gets fun, and circular—the *last* line of a pantoum is the same or nearly the same as the *first*.

For years I had a recurring dream about being lost at an airport while wearing a pair of blue shoes that belonged to my sister. Sad and confused, I kept running from terminal to terminal as blisters formed on my feet. I finally put my dream into a pantoum, and I guess it was satisfied, since it hasn't floated back into my consciousness and my feet no longer have blisters. Dreams, by the way, are *perfect* "narratives" to order into pantoums. Since dreams can often be the *furthest* from logic, they fit with that satisfying lock and key *click* into the slowed-down, repetitive quality a pantoum provides.

As soon as you wake up, catch your dream by the tail and reel it back in on the page. Images might flop around at first. That's OK. Let them flop. You can impose order and find your repeating lines later.

You, too, might sigh with relief as I often do when releasing worries over a test or feelings over a loss into a pantoum container. The pantoum can hold big emotions and will help you to move in the direction of believing that everything will be all right in the end. (It will.)

Line 1: _____

Line 2: _____

Line 3: _____

Line 4: _____

Line 5: (similar to line 2) _____

Line 6: _____

Line 7: (similar to line 4) _____

Line 8: _____

Line 9: (similar to line 6) _____

Line 10: _____

Line 11: (similar to line 8) _____

Line 12: _____

Line 13: (similar to line 10) _____

Line 14: (similar to line 3) _____

Line 15: (similar to line 12) _____

Line 16: (similar to line 1) _____

Black Belt

I wonder about the test.
Will I pass?
It's not like I haven't prepared.
My mind fills with stormy outcomes.

Will I pass?
Like a doomsday worrier, I fret.
My mind fills with stormy outcomes.
I think about the hours of exhaustion.

Like a paranoid worrier, I fret.
Sweat reaches my ears.
I think about the hours and hours of exhaustion.
I raise my fist to break the boards.

Sweat drips in my ears.
It's not like I haven't prepared.
I raise my fist to break the board.
I want this to be the last test forever.

—Josh D.

Lost (Pantoum)

You lost something important
a lost dog in the city
I lost my way in the waves
but you lost me in the trees

A lost dog in the city
a child lost in the country
but you lost me in the trees
and you lost your dog up the river

A child lost in the country
You are lost in a mall
You lost your dog up the river
You lost your mom in an accident

You lost the one you loved so much
You lost something important
You lost your mom in an accident
I lost my way in the waves.

—Josh T.

Suddenly a Story.....•

RED SOCKS AND POSTCARDS

Anytime Kat and Peter can't decide about a bookstore chore, they play a round of Rock-paper-scissors. Today, Kat's scissors cut Peter's paper, so she opens the box of new poetry books while he slinks off to work the cash register. The two pretend that bookstore near the coast where they work part-time belongs to them. Each Thursday evening, the manager lets them host a writing group on the carpet between the Fantasy and Fiction aisles. Kat creates the prompts, Peter makes the Assignments-to-Go. They pass around M&M'S and Skittles. Everyone takes turns reading what they write. No commenting is a rule. Criticism isn't invited. At the beginning of December, Peter receives a residency at a writing colony north of San Diego. The day before he leaves, he and Kat arrange a holiday display. They stack copies of Walt Whitman's *Leaves of Grass* in the window and string lights around a cardboard cutout of Emily Dickinson's face. For Peter's trip, Kat gives him a tin of oatmeal cookies and a pair of red socks tied with twine. In his first postcard, Peter tells Kat that he feels like Tom Jefferson in those socks, writing by kerosene lantern. In another postcard, he describes being at a lookout penning a poem about the sunset disguised as an angel walking backward out of heaven, the tips of his wings—which match his socks—dipping below the horizon, as crickets announce his departure.

Story Starters

- Write a postcard to a friend. Tell him or her what you're doing, reading, wearing; what's on your mind, what candy bar you last unwrapped, what wild place you want to find, to write. You *don't* have to be on vacation and you don't have to mail it.
- Create a character who loves playing games. What's his or her name? Favorite game? Last book read? Last sentence said?
- Set down a memory floating around inside your heart about someone you miss. Pretend you're with them again for an entire day. Include what you do, laugh about, play a round of Rock-paper-scissors over. Include some dialogue, let your reader overhear what's said.

Your Turn

POEM PAINTINGS

Sketch like a painter, but with words.

—Ed White to Jack Kerouac

Wander through a gallery, a museum, an artsy friend's house. Stop to *really study* each painting or picture. Linger longer at the ones that pull you in—you don't have to know or say *why* you like one over another, just let your body feel and your eyes decide which painting it wants to stay with. Then gaze a little longer.

One of my favorite poets, Pulitzer Prize–winner Lisel Mueller, wrote a poem titled "Imaginary Paintings." This poem illustrates the connection between poetry and painting, showing what close relatives they are. The Greek poet Simonides said, "Painting is silent poetry, and poetry is painting with the gift of speech." (Read this again and let it sink in.)

Many paintings, especially still lifes, are of *things*. Make note of a few things from the paintings that won't let you release your gaze, and write them on an index card. List those words that you can touch and hold with your hands (lemons, sunflowers, mice, cheese). Then attempt to paint—with words—an abstract noun: *The Future, The Past, Happiness, The Present, Love,*

Death, Hunger, The Leap of Faith, The Big Lie. In three to four lines, write how you would *paint* your abstract noun. Hint: for paint, use what you listed on your index card (oak tree, sunset, train, windowpane).

Drop Deeper

- Use brushstroked words—noun-type words, small details, natural objects, surprising and strange verbs—and take magical leaps of thought. Paint with incomplete sentences *and* broken bits of thought, use those collected words on your palette (or from your magic word tickets, see page 159). And don't forget about color. Begin with the line *How I Would Paint . . .*
- Other how-to topics: How to Make a New Color, How to Have a Happy Life, How to Get Rid of Fear, How to Build a Bridge to the Moon . . . (What else can you add to this list?)

From *Imaginary Paintings*

5. HOW I WOULD PAINT THE LEAP OF FAITH

A black cat jumping up three feet
to reach a three-inch shelf.

—Lisel Mueller

How I Would Paint Happiness

Olivia and me sitting on a freckled rock
by the oak tree in my backyard.
A walk on Throckmorton to Old Mill Park,
eating chocolate ice-cream cones.

—Emily .

How I Would Paint Death

Tears on my mother's face.
A black suit.
Throwing flower petals
onto my grandfather's grave.

—Emily

Your Turn

_____

_____

_____

_____

_____

_____

_____

_____

_____

_____

_____

_____

IDEOGRAMS

The soul never thinks without a picture.

—Aristotle

My father loved Japanese calligraphy. He kept a large sketch pad, a pot of black ink, and special-tipped calligraphy pens in a jar, on the table he made out of driftwood in our living room. Here, he sat on the floor cross-legged and practiced making the focused lines and gentle curves of kanji-stroked ideograms, where each character has its own meaning and corresponds to a particular word: flower, sun, cloud, storm. My father didn't speak or read Japanese, though he adored Zen Buddhism, sat daily in meditation, and cooked experimental dinners with seaweed, rice, fish, and a spice I still like called *gomasio*. In calligraphy he found a calm and simple beauty. Sometimes he hung his scrolls on the walls, for me and my sister to share our thoughts on what his letters looked like. "The cat about to pounce," I'd say. "It's Cupcake!" my sister would insist, the family dog our parents let her name.

Find some Chinese or Japanese characters you like. I recently found the kanji-stroked characters for *Star*, *Spirit*, and *Sunrise*. Then take a pen—a calligraphy pen, if you have one—and with the help of your writer's eye, create a little poem-story of what you might see (or hear) from a particular character's "picture." Mark Twain said, "You can't depend on your eyes when your imagination is out of focus," so focus and trust the unique way you see the world with the particular details from the connections you make—to *interpret* your experience of one chosen ideogram. It's OK to make it up. Our imaginations are *always* inviting us to loosen up and come out to play. Accept the invitation. Your ideogram might look like a hurricane approaching the coast where an osprey flies above the beach (add a description of the waves, the fish that got away, the shark approaching the shore). Another ideogram might be a crack of thunder, a curl of smoke, a spark that ignites into a flame, to light a friend's way home up a mountain.

Drop Deeper

- Pick a preposition to start one or more of your lines: Around, Behind, Below, Beyond, Between, Inside, Underneath, Throughout, Over, Near, On top of. Then *whatever* it is you see or imagine you see, write it. One student said during a poetry workshop, "Beyond the sea, on an island, in a cave, an old man with a white beard sits by a fire cleaning his calligraphy brushes, humming a song I can almost hear."

Inside the thatched-roof birdhouse
a dream sits on its nest of dream-eggs.
Inside one egg is a long-armed man
who has already learned how to juggle.
When at daybreak you hear
a little crackling sound,
look out your window and see
a brave new world, a tiny little man
juggling dark matter, nebula, stars.

—Prartho Sereno

Inside a question: echoes fly.
A teardrop of rain falls on a curved road
and blends with the lost music
below where moonlight wanders
and unasked questions
find their answers.

—Lola

Your Turn

_____

_____

_____

_____

_____

_____

_____

_____

_____

_____

_____

_____

_____

_____

_____

Mini Memoir

RIVALRY AND
SPILT SODA

Upstairs, we wait for our father. At the window we look down the broken road. I press my elbows against the ledge and tell my sister that if I lean out far enough she'll see me from the inside. Bragging, I insist I can balance out farther than she can. Only she ups the ante and insists she can free-fall. It feels like we're already falling, so I grip her skinny arms. When the phone rings, it's Dad calling to say he's on his way. I close the window, and we walk downstairs to wait. We sit on the curb and I trace the veins in my sister's arms, imagining a map that will lead us back to how our life was before, on Gordon Avenue.

Dad pulls to the curb in his blue pickup and honks twice. We jump in and he drives to a restaurant we all like. He parks, flicks off the radio, taps the dashboard, and says, *Vámonos.* The neon-green open sign winks as we walk inside. At the booth, my sister squeezes in fast while I hang back, wishing I'd edged in sooner. The waitress snaps her gum. We stare at the crease in her bosom.

Wide-eyed, my sister complains she wanted her burger *plain.* Sighing, Dad mashes his baked potato with the side of his fork while I launch into a story about my pickle being a frog with warts. Dad laughs; my sister reaches across the table and knocks her Coke into a river between us. *Jesus Christ,* Dad's voice rises, his face splotchy and red like when he catches poison oak. I offer up my napkin; my sister puckers her lips. This is our dance. Our father watches the performance. I bat my eyelashes. She sticks out her tongue. Each of us believing if we stop competing for his attention, the man ordering a slice of key lime pie might—*poof*—disappear.

Slice of Your Life

- Whose attention do you compete for? With whom do you compete? Some of my most *heated* competitions have happened with myself and my moody monkey mind.
- What are you afraid of happening? Whisper it *a slice at a time* onto the page. Don't force anything; let each word drift down at its own pace.
- Ask a parent to go on a date. What will you do? Where will you eat? Have you ever taken yourself on a date? If not, why not?

Your Turn

A NET TO GATHER YOURSELF IN

Some people are so much sunshine to the square inch.

—Walt Whitman

Look in a mirror. Pucker up. Frown. Stick out your tongue. Though you're physically all in one piece to the outward eye, have you ever had an inkling that there are parts of you— thoughts, regrets, past conversations, stories, slips of time, and mind-wanderings—hovering behind you in shimmery ether like waves?

If this question seems a bit *out there,* it is. But then again, energy moves in wonky ways through time and space. Albert Einstein called quantum physics "spooky action at a distance." My friend Elizabeth studies energy for a living. She solved her stray (spooky) energy "leakage" problem by imagining herself with a golden net that she sweeps around herself, collecting all her "signature energy" back from past events (those thoughts, regrets, past conversations, stories, slips of time, and mind-wanderings). In this way, she brings herself *entirely* into the present moment and up to speed with who she is *right now.* With her invisible golden net, Elizabeth says she untangles *her* energy particles that somehow got tangled up with *other* people's thoughts, stories, dreams, and energy particles. Her untangling efforts make her feel stronger and more clearheaded, so she can *leap deeper* into her life and into her writing, without *anything* else attached.

At first, I thought this all sounded a bit too *woo-woo weird*. That is, until I tried it with my *own* net (silver with blue flecks). It took awhile—there was *a lot* trailing behind me that needed retrieving—but guess what? It worked. I felt safer, stronger, more alive, secure, and in two words, *gathered in*. More like the clearest version of *me* again. Elizabeth's net trick transferred all my own signature energy back without anything *extra* attached. I felt like I'd been fine-tuned by a gentle lightning bolt, with my name—written in calligraphy—along the side.

And the best part of Elizabeth's invisible net trick is this: you can create *any* color net you choose. One for each day of the week. One for each outfit. Chartreuse with pink polka dots. White with turquoise stripes. Black on black. A net with an animal head or customized doodle. Dash out a description of your net, and the first thing you plan to retrieve with it. You create it, name it, use it. It's yours, as is everything you gather back with it.

Drop Deeper

- Begin by writing "I bring myself back from," and identify three or more people or places you might have gotten tangled up with. (This need not be in chronological order.)

- I bring myself back from all those camping trips with Mom, Dad, Ali—trails hiked with R.—and that date with O. when we fought about who left the bag of souvenirs on the seat of the train, pulling away from the station . . .

- Make a gift (a.k.a. an offering) of something, *anything,* to the precise moment you find yourself writing in:

I give my attention to the waning moon, hidden behind blue, a perfect sphere I know is there even if at times I do not see. I give my words to your heart, your eyes, reading this late night sentence. I whisper a friendly *Hi, how are you? Let's talk soon, share a swirl of time.*

Your Turn

FIRST AID AND SPIDERS

Be nice to people on your way up because you meet 'em
on your way down.

—Jimmy Durante

Following a water stain down the wall to the floor, Iris glimpses the spider's actual size. The guy's furry and larger than a half dollar. Holding back a shriek, she kneels to study his massive body. "Did you take a wrong turn, little buddy?" Iris likes spiders but prefers if they'd stay in their outdoor webs. Reaching for an empty water glass, she lowers it down, thinking how kind she is for not squashing him. But then he fakes left as she inches the glass in the same direction, severing one of his legs in the process. By the time they reach the window, she has severed two more. No blood, but the guy's clearly smaller than he was a few seconds ago. Prepared to fling him into the ivy, she notices he has only *four* legs instead of his born-with eight. Worried he isn't going to make it out there in his current shape, Iris looks down to study her two healthy legs and feet (and painted purple toenails). All she'd wanted was to assist him in finding his way home to his family. Impossible now *not* to think of the world's suffering and what it means to do no harm. Distressed, she releases him back into his leafy jungle and latches the window, vowing to leave the next spider she meets alone. Climbing into bed, she switches off the light and wraps herself in her comforter. Here in the dark, a poem about a certain arachnid crawls into her head.

Story Starters

- Ever try to help someone—human, reptile, animal, arachnid—only to find things unravel and shift from bad to worse? Explore an "I was just trying to help" spider-type story from your life. Begin with the sentence: *It was the kind of day that swerves . . .*
- Find a spiderweb and observe the intricacy of what a born artist created. Write whatever crawls through you, margin to margin, or put it in the shape of a web. Then switch and write from the orb-builder's point of view.

Your Turn

SHADOW WORLD

Fear has a large shadow, but he himself is small.

—*J. Ruth Gendler*

We all carry a shadow side within us, a dark part of who we *think* we are. Even when we're standing in direct sunlight. But when we turn toward and greet those parts of ourselves we don't like (or think we have to change), we might be surprised to find *a lot* of creativity stored there. Nathaniel's shadow jogs at night, plays keep-away with the moon, sprints the last mile home, and knows nothing is real. Kimiko's shadow looks for a peaceful existence and feels like a bundle of soft spiderwebs.

If you're at all curious, investigate how many layers *your* shadow has. Find out if he or she likes to wonder, wander, rip pages, leap excuses, feel the wind, taste the rain, save spiders, defy gravity, paint her toenails. . . . Think of your shadow as an imaginary friend you take on little earth journeys and beyond. (Or let your friend take you.) Wear a make-it-all-up attitude when answering the following. Have some fun as you and your shadow share a joke and locate just the right-sized meadow to stargaze and share a picnic.

Where did your shadow come from?

She dropped from the sky into the sea, swam the backstroke all
the way here to meet me in the middle of this waking dream, to
explain with a song why I must never look with calloused eyes on
anyone . . . even if he *is* dead wrong.

What questions can't your shadow touch?

What's your shadow's favorite game? Midnight snacks?

What does your shadow like to wear?

What doesn't your shadow know yet?

How does your cat or dog act around your shadow?

What's your shadow's favorite road trip? From where to where?

What tricks does your shadow perform?

What did your shadow do once? Twice? Three times? Never?

What direction does your shadow grow?

What music does your shadow listen to?

What's the scariest thing your shadow's ever done?

When and where—so far—has your shadow been the happiest?

What floats on the surface of your shadow?

What hides inside your shadow's heart?

What makes your shadow laugh?

Who does your shadow long to dance with?

Hints

- Pull a few of your shadow's answers into the light to create his or her poem. Let each image leap to the next. Forget about the way it's *supposed* to sit on the page.
- Begin with, "What you heard is true, my shadow does . . ."
- Somewhere in your poem, talk directly *to* your shadow.
- Give your shadow a pep talk. Write the way you speak.

DISAPPOINTMENT AND A LIFE RAFT

I stand under the showerhead in the upstairs bathroom and let cold water spray over my hair and neck and nightshirt. Back to bed, I run shivering and beg Sleep to carry me across her midnight channel. We're living in the sunburned apartment in Red Bluff that my father remodeled. During the day, temperatures reach 120 degrees and it feels like we're on another planet. At night, heat seeps from Main Street, rising like a fever to find me in my narrow bed on the second floor. All I want is to cast some magic spell that will turn the suffocation of our lives—Mom's anger, Dad's denial, my sister's fear, my confusion—into a breezy air-conditioned understanding. But there is no more magic left inside of me. Downstairs Mom's placing orders for her gift shop and paying bills. Upstairs my father's washing dinner dishes and filling a blue pitcher with ice water. He makes sure that we're hydrated, tucked in, safe. He sets the dial of the fan to low, tells us he loves us, then slips out for his nightly walk to the Round Up Saloon on the corner. He's only a block away, but this is the summer he'll disappear forever. In my bed, on the other side of the wall from my sister, I listen to her soft snores, along with the fan's rotating hum. With my eyes fixed on the skylight, I dream of making my escape in a life raft that's big enough to carry the girl I once was into the arms of the woman I am struggling to become.

Slice of Your Life

- Talk to the page as if it were a trusted friend. Tell it a summertime secret, a disappointed secret, a caught in-between secret, an angry-at-a-parent secret, or a wishing-your-life-was-just-plain-different secret.
- Pick a year, any year, and use it for a title. Write about one important something that happened that year. Somewhere in your writing, mention a room in your house, a chore, or a feeling on your skin (sunburn, rash, cool air, bruise).
- What does letting go feel like? Letting go feels like _____ _____ untangled from _____ and blowing in a breeze with _____ (see page 222 for feeling words for ideas).

Your Turn

ANAPHORA

naphora—a Greek word that means "carrying up or back"—was originally used in devotional poetry and indicates the *repetition* of a word or group of words that occurs at the *beginning* of a series of sentences or fragments. Anaphora is especially useful for creating a poetic effect on your ears and your reader's ears, and can intensify a poem's emotion. You can vary how many lines will start with your repeating anaphora line, and use *any* word or string of words to take anaphora for a ride into the center or out near the edge of a poem. (If you want to put the recurring line at the *end* of your phrase, this is called epistrophe.)

A painter-poet named Joe Brainard used anaphora to write an *entire* book about growing up in Oklahoma. ("I remember, downtown, whole sidewalk areas of solid grasshoppers. / I remember a shoe store with a big brown x-ray machine that showed up the bones in your feet bright green.") To write a poem with anaphora, you might use "I remember" like Joe did. Or use "The fear of" and name what you're afraid of. Even those things you don't think you *should* be afraid of at your age. (And if you're not afraid of anything, well then use I'm *not* afraid of, and head onto the open road of the page from here.)

I've heard kids your age leap off the following phrases to discover deeper truths and amuse their ears with anaphora:

I don't mind . . .   *As seen through . . .*
Here's what's so magical about . . .   *All I ever wanted . . .*
In the wilderness of . . .   *I'm caught between . . .*
It takes aeons to sculpt . . .   *Do you remember . . .*
Never mind the way . . .   *I remember . . . Because . . . You.*

You
You are
You are you
You who is you
You who is better
You who are the next best thing
You who no one can ever destroy
You who are the only one who is you
You who are my firecracker lighting up
You who are somebody who lives in this big world
You who are somebody no matter what they all say.

—Ellie

Do you remember me being sensitive
and you being tough and insensitive?
Do you remember making fun
of her pink hair? Do you remember
me being thousands of miles away?
Do you remember white butterflies
glowing in the dark like webs of light
lost in the fog, in the vast world
of time, death, and fire?

—Sara

MIRAGE

Heat of another afternoon, stretch of another humid highway, I want to be home with my friends, but my family drags me on another camping adventure, crisscrossing the entire US of A, from California to Maine and back again. Arizona, New Mexico, Oklahoma, Missouri. . . . The heat provokes me. My bare legs stick to the seat. I'm like a fork-tongued dragon, whining how miserable I am until Mom promises we'll splurge and stay in a hotel with a swimming pool and room service when we get to Ohio. Today's circled campground on the map is Land Between the Lakes Recreational Area in Kentucky. Bored out of my gourd, I can't play another round of the Alphabet Game or I Spy with my sister. The dragon inside me wants to roar for our father to *hurry up; drive faster.* Instead I slurp my dragon lips along a cherry popsicle and stare into the middle distance. When I point out the water up ahead in the road, Dad tells me, *Not yet.* The Land Between the Lakes isn't for another hundred miles. He explains again what a mirage is, the same way he reminds me about thunder and lightning, and which happens first. At home, during a storm, I count my heartbeats while my sister runs to warn our mother how close we are to bursting into flames. Now, in the rearview mirror, Dad catches the light in my dragon eyes and winks, sending me a kiss. He reaches for Mom's hand and hums a song about being lucky in love. But I know otherwise. I look out the side window

and imagine a hotel swimming pool with a slide, where I can
dive into the deep end, lose my scales, and somersault to the
bottom. Here, I'll turn back into a princess. Here, four pennies
shine, treasure I'll share with my sister. There's one coin, though,
I can't reach. When my eyelids flutter open, we're all back on the
highway, driving into the sun. The road fills with tears and like the
mirage, the fairytale I've imagined for our future shimmers, floats
off down the highway, and with a dragon's breath that matches
the sunset, disappears.

Slice of Your Life

- What / who in your life has disappeared?
- When you look up ahead, what do you see?
- What kind of year has it been—one of asking questions or answering them? What are some of the questions? What answers have you found?
- Write about a dream or retell a fairytale as though it really happened. Nowhere in your writing say: "and then I suddenly woke up."
- Do you feel more like a prince, a princess, or a dragon today?

Your Turn

WHERE IN THE WORLD?

Sail away from the safe harbor. Catch the trade winds in your sails. Explore. Dream. Discover.

—Mark Twain

There are more islands to swim toward (or away from), mountains to climb, rivers to raft, road trips to take, and countries to explore—and write in—than we have time for this trip around. Not that the fact of impermanence can stop any of us from attempting to visit as many nooks and crannies (beaches, farmers markets, dog parks, bakeries, hiking trails) on this good green-and-blue marble of a planet as we can, in the brief time we get to play here.

Here's a random list of places that I like the sound of, have been to, or dream of seeing someday. Make a list of your own place-names to track *your* travels. Begin with where you were born, including specific locations in your hometown, some of the trips you've taken, and *beyond* to where you imagine traveling in your future. Or compile a list of cities, states, and countries that begin with each letter of the alphabet. Maybe mention the mode of transportation you'll use to get there and who you'll travel with. My friend Prartho dreams of taking a pole boat down the Nile and sitting in the lap of the Sphinx surrounded by yellow sand. I once climbed the Pindus Mountains in northern Greece with a herd of sheep-friends whose tinkling bells around wooly necks led me to a secret meadow.

Sea of Cortez	Wind River Range	Pacific Crest Trail
Galapagos Islands	Honokaa, Hawaii	Papeete, Tahiti
Austin, Texas	New Orleans, Louisiana	Copenhagen, Denmark
Rockport, Maine	The Azores	Tassajara
Whidbey Island	Great Barrier Reef	Tashkent, Uzbekistan
Kyoto, Japan	Isle of Skye, Scotland	Oxford, England
Ubud, Bali	Trabia, Sicily	Mississippi Delta
Sangre de Cristo Range	Alum Rock Park	Dharamsala, India
Belize	Lake Atitlan, Guatemala	Costa Rica
The Bering Sea	New York City	Ho Chi Minh City
Plateau of Tibet	Painted Desert, Arizona	The Moon

Surprise Yourself Survey

PUT YOUR COURAGE ON THE PAGE

But have the courage to write whatever your dream
is for yourself.

—May Sarton

It takes oodles of courage to write and to keep writing when we bump up against those jagged places *inside* that make us cringe, cause our heart to shudder, twist, tremble, crack, and break open—you know, the places that smell musty and feel like they swarm with bloodsucking bats. You also know that you *have* to go in there, to face down the bats (and dragons) and shine a brave beam of light on to your fear. *But why?* you ask. Because *that's* the only way to release the *huge* amount of trapped energy that you need to fuel your writing.

You don't have to answer every question from every Surprise Yourself Survey; just choose a few and follow where your answers lead. With as much courage as you can muster, make sense or not. Combine the answers that hold the most magic, truth, and, yes, even a dark fear or two. Where you risk the most will reveal something new you never knew you knew.

What if, across a distant valley, my voice turns into:

a vine, then into the tight weave of a rickety bridge that I have to
talk myself across, inch by inch, my life echoing out across time's
valley as I sit down beside you at a diner in the sky, share a slice of
key lime pie, find out why you left, why you had to die.

Today, I want nothing more than: _____

Inside my cave of fear, I find these what-if questions:

_____

Unfastening the line of reason, here's what's no longer impossible:

_____

If I wasn't scared, this is the first place I'd travel: _____

If I dive into the center, I might find: _____

Stacked at the bottom of my heart is: _____

Shoved to the side is: _____

Standing in plain sight is: _____

Wanting my attention is: _____

One day I might discover: _____

SKIPPING AND BROKEN BITS OF TRUTH

Life is a whim of several billion cells to be you for a while.

—*Groucho Marx*

Forget who might be watching and find a sidewalk, strip of grass, long driveway, or deserted runway. Then skip. Come on, you know you want to. Skipping past a certain age is *way* underrated. If someone gives you a funny look or asks what you're doing, tell them it's for a creative-writing experiment. Tell them that you *have* to. Then skip for at least five minutes. Feel your way *into* what it's like to be free, like a wild horse or an uncaged bird, wind in your hair, elevating off the earth minus any buzzing worries and stinging cares.

Then pace your writing the way you skip. For those who are used to writing in complete sentences, this means the *opposite*. Write in fragments, in broken bits of thought. For some of us this can be challenging. Especially if you've been in school awhile and have that complete-sentence-rule thing drilled through your head. Just for today, drop all thoughts of right and wrong. Break the rules. Rip a page out of the heart's only rule book, and risk loving what you love—and while you're at it, *who* you love, too. Then write a few or few hundred fragments about your life, *after* the skip. As you know it. Right now. Say what's so. It won't hurt. Pinky-swear.

Drop Deeper

- Peer from a distance and become the *He* or *She* of a broken bit of your life and write in the third person, in sentence fragments: *To the market she skips. Late in the afternoon. Where sun slants through. Scent of eucalyptus. An expanding worldview. Artichokes, yes. Pulled pork, never. Sits on beaches. Counts Saturn's rings. Rescues hurt birds, lost memories, stray words.*
- What does it feel like to skip or gallop? Or do you need to explore the problem of having *forgotten* how to skip?

Prayer

Our problem—may I include you?—is that we
don't know how to start, how to just close
our eyes and let something dance between
our heart and our lips. We don't know how
to skip across the room only for the joy of the leap.
We walk, we run, but what happened to the skip
and its partner the gallop, the useless and imaginary
way we could move through space, the horses we
rode before we knew how to saddle up, before we
had opinions about everything and just loved
the wind in our faces and the horizon in our eyes.

—Stuart Kestenbaum

Your Turn

FRUSTRATION AND A WING TIP

Through early morning air, B. J. returns. Clive, unaware, eats his breakfast of high protein crunchies then saunters across the patio to greet the day in his usual tigerlike way. By the fuchsia, he claims his place in the flower bed and begins the daily ritual of cleaning his forepaws. There, above the lowest branch of the sycamore, B. J. perches . . . then up on the fence . . . then back in the sycamore. B. J.'s frenzied flight: the cause of Clive's whiskered concern. *Hey, what the *α%∧!* Clive mews. Inside, the house fills with getting-ready-for-school sounds. Oatmeal bubbles on the back burner, a clatter of cups, bowls, spoons punctuates the usual question from down the hall, *Anybody seen my homework?* Clive, however, has bigger problems to solve. All at once, B. J. swoops, brushing the fur of his back with her wing tip. Turning, Clive raises a claw and chatters openmouthed at the daring jay. *What the *%α!!? You've got nerve, crazy bird!* Clive yowls. B. J. caws: *Stay away from my nest, fat cat.* No one wants to break it to the eighteen-pound feline. If any of us turned into a bird and spotted his gray-and-white rotundness beneath a tree, housing *our* nest, we'd do exactly the same thing.

Story Starters

- Pay attention to an animal and observe his or her minute-to-minute life. Where does he prowl? Eat? Sleep? What do you imagine he hears in the dark? Translate a few looks that this animal cannot speak.
- Write a poem from the nine wild lives of your cat. Or the one spastic point of view of your dog.
- Feel the wind rush around you, spread your fingers wide like the quills of flight feathers, become a bird on the page—swoop, dive, plummet—into a blur. Where do you fly? What is it like to forget your two-legged life?

Your Turn

ANIMAL LANGUAGE

"Meow" means "woof" in cat.

—George Carlin

Write a story using as many animal sounds as possible. Let there be a conflict right at the beginning. A bird, say, who has laid her eggs in a nest in a tree. A tribe of cats, circling the trunk below. It's OK to make up words for the sounds you hear. Just be sure to translate for your real and imaginary animal characters. Or create a poem where each line or sentence uses the name of a different animal or animal sound. Here are the first five lines of Ronald Wallace's poem "In a Rut":

She dogs me while
I try to take a catnap.
Of course, I'm playing possum but
I can feel her watching me,
eagle-eyed, like a hawk

In thirty more lines the rest of the narrative unfolds. It's worth finding to read how the characters call each other animal names on every line. For animal name ideas, see page 204.

Barking	Hissing	Drool
Splashing	Rustling of quills	Tumble
Chatters	Ringing	Lunge
Grunts	Deep howling	Chase
Panting	Whinny calls	Nudge
Gurgles	Trumpeting roars	Race
Deep purrs	Laughing	Swipe
Howling	Cooing	Running
Wailing	Growling purrs	Nipping
Shrill yapping	Bleating	Guarding
Snarling screams	Meowing	Begging
Hums	Sqwawking	Sniffing
Drumming	Snorting	Snarling
Grumbling	Yelping	Retrieve
Whistling	Braying	Pounce
Soft roaring	Deep yapping	Lick
Growls	Grunts	Fetch
Purrs	Mumbled growls	Nap
Grunting roars	Shrill calls	Muzzle

ENDANGERED SPECIES

The greatness of a nation and its moral progress can be
judged by the way its animals are treated.

—Mahatma Gandhi

I heard on BBC *Nature News* that a fifth of animals without
backbones could be at risk of extinction. A fifth! Sad to say,
the list on the next page is only a *small* fraction of the mammals,
birds, reptiles, fish, insects, amphibians, snails, clams, arachnids,
crustaceans, and worms sharing life on our tilted planet that are
currently endangered and in need of help. Not to mention all
the corals, jellyfish, sea anemones, and centipedes that are also
disappearing. (Deep sigh.) Perhaps writing a poem for one of the
following will let other well-intentioned two-leggeds know what's
at stake, *before* it's too late, so we don't have only poems left to
remember what a species once meant to us.

To what length would you go to befriend one of the following? Write a letter *directly* to this animal, apologizing, reassuring,
detailing what *you* will do to lend a human hand.

Virgin Island Tree Boa
Serpent Island Centipede
Gopher Frog
Bearded Screech Owl
Azorean Bat
Gray Wolf
Central Rock Rat
Egyptian Vulture
American Crocodile
Kauai Cave Wolf Spider
Lotis Blue Butterfly
Indian Python
Rainbow Parrotfish
Black-Spotted Newt
Alabama Red-Bellied Turtle
Baja California Legless Lizard
Tree Hole Crab
Ivory-Billed Woodpecker
Jaguar

Brazilian Three-Toed Sloth
African Slender-Snouted Crocodile
Earthworm
Mt. Hermon June Beetle
Speartooth Shark
Asian Elephant
Banded Hare-Wallaby
Cascade Caverns Salamander
Brown Bear
Black-Snouted Flying Frog
Alabama Beach Mouse
Armored Snail
Burmese Peacock Turtle
Saiga Antelope
Badplaas Black Millipede
Black-Striped Sportive Lemur
Maldives Fruit Bat
Bush Dog
California Condor

POEMS BEHIND YOUR KNEES

The body is the starting place for what we know.
—Dorianne Laux

Take a walk or a bike ride. Around the block. Down a flight of bleachers (interesting on a bike; safer on foot). Across a vacant lot, up a mountain, over a meadow, and through the woods—saving the visit to Grandmother's house for later. Stay out long enough to get your heart pumping. Pay attention to the air temperature swirling around your face and ears; the swing of your arms, hip sway, foot placement. Listen to which part of your body is talking the loudest. Does the belly of your hamstrings whine out a song or scream? Do elbows, wrists, hands, fingers hum, thanking you for giving them a break from gripping lead-filled sticks and maneuvering a mouse around? Do toes, soles, heels of your feet wonder, *Why didn't you take us out sooner?* No need to answer. All you have to do is *listen*.

Once you tune in to the voice of your body, find out *which* body part has *more* to say. A poem could be waiting inside your right elbow, the clench of your jaw, grit of your teeth, or working its way through your left or right knee (my left knee has *a lot* to say).

There's bound to be a poem in your neck, the space around your ribs, or in the soles of your devoted feet that carry you around our hard-surfaced world. Record compliments, complaints, cooped-up demands, any long-held plans, fears, sadnesses, gratitudes, annoyances, preferences. Your body knows the truth. It doesn't lie. If you get still enough, it might even read your mind.

Drop Deeper

- List five body parts and five questions you'd ask if parts of your body could talk . . . then conduct an interview.
- Take note of the small movements you make every day: putting on an earring, bending for a tennis ball, cradling the cat, twirling a forkful of spaghetti . . . Keep going! What do you grasp for? Pull at? Lean into . . .? Choose a few to include in a poem titled "Dance," and then perform it.

End-of-Day Dance

The floss-sway of string, a minty back and forth;
the scrub of the face, the tucked-lock-of-hair
behind each pearl-dotted ear; the talk of my tongue,
the search for my book; the twitch of Roo's tail,
the hum of her purr, first felt and now heard.
The crease of our brains, the expanse of each rib,
the dance of this day as we fold into bed.

—Carolyn Ingram

Your Turn

_____

_____

_____

_____

_____

_____

_____

_____

_____

_____

_____

_____

_____

_____

_____

MIMICKING MOVEMENT

Learning is movement from moment to moment.

—*Jiddu Krishnamurti*

If we can bypass our mind, our body will tell us the truth of how we're *really* feeling. Movement can bring out what we most need to say. If your guard's up, wiggle around until it's lowered. If you're shy, close your eyes. Then move for a solid minute *any way* your body needs and wants to shift, stir, spin, change position. Use the range and reach of your *entire* being's dance to mimic the technique of rain, light breaking, the growth of a tree, a moth flying toward a flame, the heart of something brave, a winter morning, a curtain closing on something you still want to see.

Pick the movement your body most enjoyed mimicking and write "It feels like" at the top of your page. Then transform the movement into words. Keep coming back to "It feels like" or another anaphora line (see page 187 for anaphora examples). Repetition can help you drop in and tunnel deeper into meaning.) There's no right or wrong way to do this, just as there's no right or wrong way to move. You're creating something *entirely* your own out of the one-of-a-kind way your body wheels, kicks, prances, lunges, lifts off, and flies. Trust this. Translate your movements into words with or without making sense, and you're home free. Hint: similes help. My hands drift like . . . my feet rise like . . . my arms sway like. . . my head moves back and forth like. . . my legs lunge like.

Drop Deeper

* Let your pen dance down the page, roll forward and back in time, as you shift into *any* memory, anticipation, state of being, place in nature that lets something new bloom inside of you. Let it even take you to a place you *don't* want to go. *But why would I want to do that?* you ask. Because there's probably *a lot* of energy and originality waiting for you there.
* How does lightning write itself into a poem? What about thunder? A tornado? A tsunami? A monsoon? (What gets spit out? Refused? Called back? Rocked? Held?)

Lightning fistfights with the sky
punches left, swerves right—
back and forth like a boxer
on steroids. Spits out yellow
then white, refuses to back down . . .
falls quiet when thunder
screams out or cries.

—*group response*

Your Turn

On-the-Spot Drop

THE MAP OF
YOUR HAND

You cannot shake hands with a clenched fist.
—Indira Gandhi

Study your knuckles, palm lines, fingers, thumbs. Fold your hands into a tepee or a steeple. Massage your scalp. Untie a knot. Scratch your dog's itchy back. Grip a pen, jot a note, shoot some hoops, dip a spoon into a cup of soup, doodle a few loop-de-loops. Lend a hand and hand it over, handsome. I read somewhere that you must "put your heart in your hands when you write," so press your hands together, prayer-like, whisper an intention to your palms and fingers, and imagine your heart, here with you, as you write.

A palm-reader friend told me that the hands represent the part of us that shapes our lives. Our dominant hand shows what we've done and where we're headed; the nondominant hand presents what we brought into this life. By using your hands to hold a sharpened pencil rather than pushing fingers down on lettered keys or, with thumbs, dashing out another text, the anxiety that gets trapped in your mind and body has a chance to calm, unwind, loosen, release. When you set words onto a page, a path around your heart naturally opens and clears. This strengthens your relationship with yourself (and friends, family, acquaintances, even total strangers). Put your life, words, details, images in good hands—your *own*.

Drop Deeper

- Name a few or a few hundred things that your hands have had the pleasure (or pain) of touching, what they remember reaching for, holding, releasing. What waits or hangs *beyond* their grasp?
- Be your own palm reader. Make up what each line, freckle, vein, scar, hangnail, or birthmark represents or is linked to. (The freckles on my writing hand form a small constellation; my writer's bump on my middle finger is a hill of pride; my veins link me to my sweet Sicilian grandmother whose veins bulged from strong hands too.) Be far-fetched, stick to the facts, reveal your act. Finish these lines:

  That's the scar from _____ . Here is the

  road where my writer's bump _____ . This

  is the intersection between _____ and _____

  _____ .

- Make a portrait of your hands or someone else's hands. What do they cling to, discover, pick up, unlatch? Or combine *two* hand portraits like Charlie did.

Palm Reader (For My Father)

My small hands clung to his massive sausage fingers.
His hands provided support for my fallen body.
My hands discovered the meaning of pain.
His hands picked me up again.
My hands, like god's speedometer, made no coherent sense.
His hands cleverly unlatched that dysfunctional crib,
releasing me for the umpteenth time.
Here's the avenue with two forks in the road.
Here's the intersection at the center where I return free.

—Charlie

Your Turn

BONES, ORGANS, LIGAMENTS, OH MY

Take care of your body. It's the only place you have to live.

—Jim Rohn

Beyond what we groom, bathe, polish, and brush, beyond our arms, legs, feet, and hands, our body contains 206 bones, which make up our skeletons, without which we'd flop around like blobs of jelly. The tiniest bone, the stirrup, lives inside our ear and is just three millimeters long. The longest, the femur, is in the leg. The largest is the thick and sturdy thighbone. We have more than 600 muscles, the most powerful of which are located along our spines (so no slumping or slouching, please!). There are 78 organs in our body, each of which plays a specific role *and* works with the others to keep us alive *and* writing. Aren't we lucky? I mean, what if we'd been born as slugs? (No offense to slugs.)

Find *one* body part in the list below that you've *never* heard of (or maybe have heard of, but have *no clue* what function it performs for you). I recently fell while playing a friendly pickup game of soccer with a group of ten-year-olds. (I really wanted that goal!) The MRI X-ray showed I'd snapped my anterior cruciate ligament in two places. *My what?* I asked the handsome surgeon who replaced my ACL with a hamstring from a cadaver. Select a body part you've *never* seen or heard of, and conduct a little in-ves-ti-ga-tion as to how it works to keep you upright, active, alive, able to swallow, flex, swivel, bend, breathe. After all, this body that houses your spirit belongs to you, or at least it's on loan for a while. Write *directly* to a part of your body, a note in the form of an ode (a poem of praise). Sing it a song on the spot. Prove you don't take your tibia, pancreas, ulna, scapula—or anything else for that matter—for granted.

Coccyx	Pancreas	Deltoid
Fibula	Basal ganglia	Sacrum
Tibia	Thorax	Lumbar vertebrae
Clavicle	Cerebellum	Talus
Humerus	Hypothalamus	Thoracic vertebrae
Ulna	Scapula	Adenoids
Adrenals	Maxilla	Spleen
Trachea	Mandible	Occipital ridge
Amygdala	Metatarsal	Trapezius
Navicular	Phalange	Hyoid

SPY

I follow the smell of turpentine downstairs and tiptoe across the landing. In the corner, near a stack of lumber, I bend down and peek into the family room. My mother's sitting on the wide-planked floor that she refinished. She's wearing a gray T-shirt and her garage-sale jeans with the cuffs rolled up, her hair held back with a blue bandana. The way she rests on her heels makes me think of a bird, perched before flight. My father's leaning against the brick wall that he sandblasted, an unlit cigarette wedged between two fingers of his right hand. Tension fills the air, though you can't see it since it's hiding, like me. I have felt this tension for years but can't yet match it with words. The way my mother sighs makes my heart race like when I practice earthquake drills in elementary school, and duck down to take cover under my desk.

"It's nothing," my father assures. He reminds her he has other friends besides his *drinking buddies*. He smiles his handsome smile then strikes a match to light his cigarette. He's as skilled a carpenter as he is at finding his way out of a direct question, without my mother noticing the nail holes or seeing the glue. He has a way of changing things around—and not just rooms in a house. He can change words and shades of meaning, too. He used to stay at home with me and my sister when we lived on Gordon Avenue and he was between jobs. He'd make tuna fish sandwiches for lunch, remembering to cut mine diagonally without the crusts and to leave my sister's whole. He'd let us take naps in the living room with pillows off the couch and help us build forts using sheets and blankets from the linen closet. Later, we'd pile into his pickup and shop for groceries at the Mexican market downtown. For dinner he'd make chicken enchiladas, Mom's favorite, with guacamole and salsa, refried beans, homemade corn tortillas, and a salad I picked the artichoke hearts out of. He'd blend a pitcher of margaritas and put extra salt around the rim of Mom's glass. Back then, my mother didn't think to ask him how he spent his afternoons. She got home from work, slipped off her shoes, and found him in the kitchen humming. She'd sneak up behind him, put her hands over his eyes, and whisper *Guess who?* She'd kiss him on the mouth for a long time, when she thought my sister and I weren't looking.

Still hiding, I sweep sawdust with my fingertips into four small mounds and smooth them down. I find a nail and lightly trace each of our names across the new floor as my parents make a decision that will forever change our lives.

Slice of Your Life

* Who got divorced? Where were you when you found out?
* Write about what each of your parents does. Write about what *you* want to do.
* Who have you spied on? What did you overhear?

Your Turn

RIGHT, WRONG, GOOD, BAD . . . BLAH, BLAH, BLAH

Write about what makes you different.

—Sandra Cisneros

C heck all judgments at the door. You know, *good, bad, right, wrong, smart, stupid.* . . . Leave all expectations, obligations, *shoulds, oughts, musts,* and *have tos* heaped on the floor. They'll be waiting for you at the end of this book, if you want to pick them up.

Now wipe off your hands, take a breath, and make some bare assertions. No explaining. No complaining. Just write a clean sentence about *whatever* you happen to see, hear, taste, smell, feel. Right now. *Whatever* you are or aren't doing, say what you want, what you lost, what you overheard, do or don't recognize as lonely fact, whispered opinion, pure fiction, *without anything else attached.* Now's your chance to swap all those pesky *shoulds* for cuddly *coulds*, all those wadded-up *have tos* for crinkle-free *get tos.*

Take a lion's breath—inhale through the nose, exhale through the mouth, stick out your tongue, and say *ahhhh*—and just notice what you notice. Record your first five observations, then go for five more, and five more after that. No need to defend, qualify, use "because," trot out your rehearsed, made-up, or wild reasons why. I know, right? *What* a relief.

Here are five observations that I wrote down on the first day of fall. *I don't want my grandmother to die. I ate a sweet potato for lunch. Prayer flags make me happy. Collin and I listened to* A Wrinkle in Time *driving home from Berkeley. Clive caught a hummingbird and left it on the welcome mat.*

Drop Deeper

* Create a poem made *entirely* of one-sentence detailed assertions like Lesle Lewis does in "Red Bank." Write it entirely in the past tense. (I wanted, jumped, recognized, lived, saw, lost, didn't.) Make up at least one assertion. End by finishing the line, "Definitely, I am not _____."
* Name everything and anything you miss.

Red Bank

I wanted a horse.
I jumped from a plane.
I was not comfortable with your illness.
I was a detective at the wedding.
I recognized the new way it would be with you in rehabilitation.
I saw how the sunset colors on the Navesink River got sad
     with the lone rower.
I lived on a lone planet of befuddlement.
I'd lost a person.

I didn't know how to hold my lips.
I was like the goose bathing in parking lot puddles.
Definitely, I am on a train.

—Lesle Lewis

What I Miss

I miss Mom at the head of the table, Dad
across from me, Matthew at the end,
and Dashiell right beside me.
That feeling of apart is like two halves
instead of one whole.
I don't miss being asked,
"Which house are you going to today?"
I miss having one whole home.
I miss when my mom wore a ring.
I miss when my parents never fought.
I miss that bliss I believed in once.

—Lily

Your Turn

_____

_____

_____

_____

_____

_____

_____

WORDS TO SAY WHAT AND HOW YOU FEEL

You owe reality nothing and the truth about
your feelings everything.

—*Richard Hugo*

C rack open a way you've felt in the last month, week, day, minute. Feelings are just energy that longs to be experienced, through the dips and spikes of our gravity-ruled life. Feelings, in my experience, can and do rise to the surface in both joyful *and* complicated pairs . . . and can sometimes be challenging to pin down and name. "The clear expression of mixed feelings" is what the poet W. H. Auden called poetry.

Find *any* words and *any* descriptions that take you to the heart of what you're feeling. This needn't make sense or be tidy. Feelings can be a messy, mixed-up bunch. (Perhaps check out the list of animal sounds to get started, on page 202.) Sometimes I combine pairs of feelings into layers: *That "trapped in a maze of my own making and happy that I can't escape" my book deadline feeling. The "I'm so excited to be hanging out with Collin eating sushi rolls yet missing something (someone) I can't name" feeling. That "how come he's not paying attention to me anymore" quick lash of jealousy feeling.* There's also the "simile feelings": *I feel like a pond without fish feeling. I feel like a mountain without wind feeling.* You get the picture.

It takes practice to feel and name your feelings as they do their swirly-twirly, do-si-do dance through you. But as you practice, it *does* get easier, until you automatically feel more alive and spacious inside. The alternative—bottling your feelings up and leaving them to sit on dusty shelves—tends not to work so well. (I've tried it, I know.) Write a few sentences about a time you felt something complicated, like excitement mixed with fear or a tinge of embarrassment mixed with tears. Include where in your body you felt this (neck, throat, chest, stomach), and maybe who you were with when the feeling surfaced. A middle-school-aged friend was feeling that excitement/embarrassment combo last week in her throat and on her cheeks when she spotted this guy from her swim team at the frozen yogurt shop. She wanted to stop and say hi, ask about the peanut-butter vanilla special, his backstroke, *anything* to be near him, hear his voice say her name, but, well, she felt too starlit giddy and shy around the edges to move a step in his direction. Has this ever happened to you? If so, what did you do? Circle a few combinations on the next page, and venture into sharing some of your wanting-to-say-hi-to-the-cute-guy-at-the-yogurt-shop type feelings.

giddy and scared
hot and loud
slippery and loose
deep and silent
jittery and excited
frozen and sad
burning and eager
achy and breaky
nervous and irritated
tingly and stiff
hidden and hollow
knotted-up and shy
balanced and trusting
rainy and moonless
echo-filled and starlit
stormy and scattered
wolflike and moon-filled
rocklike and secretive

gusty and whirling
rippled and rejected
rooted and proud
locked up and thirsty
jumpy and optimistic
floaty and winged
reflective and intuitive
dreamy and dancey
hungry and sleepy
careful and caught
heart-filled and changed
mossy and mindful
thankful and peaceful
silly and eager
generous and terrified
snobby and lost
gentle and surprised
lonely and shattered

tearful and brave
crazed and concerned
beautiful and bendy
embarrassed and proud
rushed and confused
beamish and show-offy
cute and hyper
smashing and smitten
mean and toothy
brilliant and bookish
greedy and shameful
smelly and courageous
hermit-like and happy
whimsical and loved
icicle-like and wanting
creative and joyous
tender and bruised
tangled-up and annoyed

ASSERT YOUR NOS; FIND YOUR YESES AND WOWS

The big question is whether you are going to be able to say a hearty yes to your adventure.

—Joseph Campbell

I n one of the several books I'm in the middle of reading—I tend to juggle more than one story at a time—it says that there are really only three responses *to* the world: *No, Yes,* and *Wow.* If your world is feeling stuck, toss *No* over the side and reverse course into the land of *Yes.* If you're overwhelmed by how much you're doing and agreeing to, consider swapping *Yes* for the simple and astonished *Wow* for a spell. In the list on the next page, say *No* to everything you *aren't* going to write about, then find your authentic and absolute *Yes* lights—even your *Wow* panel—and take up writing from here.

Give the page three odd, yet precise details about the next place you wander and the next person you see.

- With the next step I'm on the Metro in Paris, off to meet a friend at Shakespeare and Company Bookstore, when I see that musician in the red plaid jacket playing his accordion. A few notes of "Moon River," and he passes me his beret. What will life hand me next? Where will life take this guy?

Write about the last time you laughed so hard that a slurp of soda came out your nose. Somewhere include your name, an object from your grandmother's house, and the condiment you like least (*mayonnaise—yuck!*).

Your life is a treasure trove. What three things (in daring detail) would you like to keep forever from this stash? Somewhere use a few of the following words: *mumbo jumbo, wildebeest, confetti, speed racer, jackknife, red-bellied, fortune-teller, headfirst.* Use them as nouns or verbs.

So, where were you today? Answer this question in either a guilty or innocent tone, but don't use the words *guilt* or *innocence* in your writing. Do mention an ice cream flavor you haven't tried (yet), some feeling state—joy, hunger, regret, anticipation—or a sound you heard within the last hour (*pen strokes on paper, a whirling fan, a knock at the door*).

What magic moments happened today? Quick images, small fragmented moments are fine. Begin with "I remember." Somewhere mention a small creature, an object you use every day (*a fork, a toothbrush, a key*), and the month or season you were born.

Attach a color (middle-of-the-night blue, the hushed hue of silver, flirty pink) to your mood today, and fill in the details of this sentence: *Never in my wildest dreams did I imagine this could happen.*

Choose three simple objects from the room where you are right now. Write about one of the objects, but *don't* mention what it is.

Fine to mention the other two. Include the weather of the room (tense, welcoming, calm, angry, flat, full, bland, ripe, blooming).

In *The Lord of the Rings* Bilbo Baggins says, "Not all those who wander are lost." Where do you wander without feeling lost? Somewhere mention a direction, a time of day, a road sign—*no trespassing, blind curve ahead, speed limit 100 mph*—plus your favorite shape, fruit, and vegetable.

Finish this line: *Once upon a time, I didn't* . . . Somewhere drop in a day of the week, an animal sound, and a body part you know the name and function of (see page 214).

Begin with the line: *Everyone knows how that story ends* . . ., then tell the story, real or imagined. Somewhere mention something you're afraid of, the word *happiness*, the smallest object you can imagine, or something you pry open *(a pistachio shell, a lid on a jar of honey, your heart . . .)*.

Start and end a description of a close friend—include the sound of his voice, her eye color, his most often worn article of clothing, plus something memorable you remember her saying. Oh, and be sure to mention his favorite condiment *(mayonnaise, yum!)*.

SYLLABIC VERSE

If you like to count, you'll probably enjoy putting your poems into syllabic verse. This is a poetic form that *purposely* has a fixed number of syllables per line. An American poet named Marianne Moore *loved* to count syllables and gave herself little tasks in her poems, such as "This poem shall have seven syllables per line, with the exception of three lines that will have only five syllables." Moore believed that the most important thing about a poem is "precise heartfelt expression" and was able to achieve this for herself by writing in syllabic verse. But in the event syllabic verse doesn't float your poetic boat, she also said, "Poetry is a matter of skill and honesty in *any* form." In her most famous poem, titled "Poetry," she hoped for poets who could produce "imaginary gardens with real toads in them." I *never* tire of reading this line, and only wish I had known Moore, who adored sports, wore a black cape and tricorn hat, *and* got to throw out the first pitch for the 1968 season in Yankee Stadium. She had *that* sort of style. She was *that* lucky. Oh, and she also admired Muhammad Ali and had a baseball signed by Mickey Mantle! Doesn't she sound like someone *you'd* like to take a walk with down a long city sidewalk? Or simply create—and count—a few lines of a poem with?

Zoe wrote this poem after cat Clive was hit by a car on his way home from hunting one morning. She didn't intend for it to be a perfect syllabic poem, but that's what it turned into.

Count the syllables per line and find out.

Clive

grey and white wonder
hunter and roamer
hummingbird pouncer
tangler with skunker
salmon-boy slurper
super-smooth yowler
moment wide moodler
lengthwise sun-napper
outer space starer
padded paw cruiser
future car dodger

—Zoe

My friend Albert plays with syllabics by tipping his phone number on its side in the margin, then writing a poem with the same number of syllables to correspond to each digit. Just for fun, use your phone number to match the number of syllables you'll allow yourself to use. Or use your phone number to equal the number of *words* you place on each line. If your telephone number is 550–4347, your poem might be (counting syllables):

Let me into your
Little silver hut
Oh—
Don't close the door
No, no, no
The shimmer-light's
where we are all forever.

Mini Memoir

BOARDING A BUS

The end of her freshman year of high school, my sister starts counting calories. One apple = 50 calories. One skinless chicken breast = 142 calories. Pretty soon she flat-out refuses to eat much of anything. At five feet eight inches, she weighs ninety pounds and has to leave to live in a hospital in San Francisco. I'm away at college with swarms of confusing feelings following me as I walk in Ugg boots to my English classes in Taylor Hall. In every poem I write, I imagine what my sister is living through. I feel as fragile as a spiderweb, our lives too entangled on the inside to unravel.

On the outside it looks like this: I board a bus to San Francisco and get off in front of the hospital on the medical center campus. I stare up, at the square-paned lights on the fourth floor. I watch as other people's lives drift by. I've arrived too late, visiting hours have ended. An arm of fog reaches across the city, and all I want is to break my sister out of the hell she has been admitted to. I want to believe if I perform one daring act, everything will be put back as it was before—our father's eyes in the rearview mirror, our mother repeating the stories we love, my sister asleep on the seat beside me; our years as a family continuing to unfold. Instead I search my backpack for a pen. I look for the right words to unlock the doors that have closed between us. In the lobby, a nurse lets me leave a note along with a pack of Mambas, my sister's favorite candy. I want to stay. I have to go. I make my solo escape into the fog and cross street after street of horns and headlights.

After college, I'll move to San Francisco, but by then my sister will be living somewhere else. All you have is right now, I hear myself say, *a place on the sidewalk, at the corner of Cole and Carl.* I wait here until another bus rolls to the curb, and I watch each passenger step off, all the men who remind me of my father, my heart beating *stop, stop* as I wish one of my childish wishes: *let me cast a magic spell, to pause time long enough to piece together what has happened to us.* But I can't stop time or stop anyone from leaving. Not even myself. So I board that bus, take a seat by the window, and ride via the present into my future.

Slice of Your Life

- Each day we leave behind our past and ride into our future. Think of something important—a move, a new school, the loss of a best beloved, something huge you're traveling through on your way to the other side. If you're not sure, launch from: "What I really want to say is . . ." (a line from one of my writing teachers, Natalie Goldberg). As soon as you start writing, you'll be transported to the *exact* spot you need to be. (Go back to this line as often as you like.)
- What's something you think you can't do? Go there on the page and write as though you've *already* done it.
- Be brave, leap off: "I'm not going to write about . . ." (That's the line I used to start this mini memoir.)

Your Turn

WHAT THEY TELL YOU TO FORGET

There's a crack in everything. / That's how the light gets in.
—*Leonard Cohen*

Reach for something easy—a shell, a brownie—then set it down. Or eat it—the brownie, not the shell. Then graduate to something medium-heavy—this book, that houseplant. Then something heavier—your backpack, a chair, the cat. Think of all the things (or thingamagigs) you've picked up and carried around over the course of your unfolding life. The physical things you just lifted *and* the rules and teachings from others, even the emotions and memories you tote around in the shoe box of your heart where light can't always reach until you open the lid and peer inside. As creative writers we learn to get comfortable with peering in and seeing the cracks—and the light—in everything.

Has anyone ever said to you, *Aw, forget about it. Put it out of your mind. Don't give it another thought.* Sometimes this advice works. Other times you might find yourself *longing* for that one friend who knows to sit there and just listen. That friend who will hold their phone calls, cancel all appointments, and step off the busy ride of life to simply *listen,* without commenting or telling you what to do. That person you can trust by the soft focus of his eyes. The friend who lets you go on talking (and sighing) for as long as you need.

If you don't have that person handy today, you do have the page. And the page won't ever say, *Come on, already, push past it.* It's really OK to write (and speak) what they tell you to forget. I do it all the time. *You* get to say when you're finished. You decide when you're all through.

Drop Deeper

- How would you express your most tender self using the word *like* followed by a series of objects? *(Like eggshells, like the cat's breath against my wrist, like jeweled pomegranate seeds, like a lost shoestring, like wind in a canyon . . .)* Go for a series of similes to match your age. I made five above, only forty-one more to go.
- Whether you're uncertain over a small or huge decision—which cupcake flavor to choose, which parent to live with—include everything you want to say, fake, fast-forward, rewind, erase. Include what you never told anybody, if you're feeling especially brave. Go to that dark place inside and let in some light. You have spirals of time. There's no need to rush or hurry (ever).

All I ever wanted was to be heard, recognized.
Instead I'm stuck doing the dishes
and making my bed every morning.
Okay, so the truth is nobody gets what they want.
Like how I wanted a new phone. Did I get it? Heck, no.
Sometimes it seems like I'm abandoned, left behind.
I don't know where to turn next, feel I'm walking an endless path.
I never told anyone about your secret. That secret
about how you saw it, how you heard it,
how you felt it. Here's the look that says it all:
You should probably shut your mouth unless
you want to get smacked across the face.
I hate that look. Every thought is lost
until I focus on you. It's like I can read your mind.
I feel your pain. I share your laughter.

—Maia

Your Turn

THE SUM OF ALL FEELING

'Tis the privilege of friendship to talk nonsense,
and to have her nonsense respected.

—Charles Lamb

Finish only the lines below that you know you *won't* be tempted to make sense of. Forget the rest. Really. Making sense (unless you absolutely have to) can be overrated when you're out to loosen the grip of your inner critic. Even if you only answer one line from this survey, that's OK. Remember: you're amazing *and* starlit, a genius at living your life—even when your equations don't involve precise math or telling the exact time. (Of course, if you need to make linear sense, who am I to stop you?)

The sum of a cicada's song + the edge of midnight =

the summer we hiked that gorge to the sea, the indigo sky filled with insect sounds, your headlamp guiding us around juniper and fir trees, our conversation and laughter intertwined through the long shadow of our childhood, how you assured me we'd both be fine.

A light beam opens into that time when: _____

A deserted beach + two clouds = _____

Here's the look that says: _____

Hills of school + a smudge of blackness = _____

_____

My best friend keeps asking me if: _____

Each shiver + every minute = _____

This is what is written in the sand: _____

A stone in my hand + a wide river = _____

Sometimes the only thing that softens the edges is: _____

_____

Love for my life + a fist of feathers = _____

Inhaling I take the world in, exhaling I give back: _____

_____

Bonus

Collect two facts and/or odd bits of truth you learned last week. Combine them into a poem with a few lines from above. If you'd like, somewhere add those plus and equal signs.

STOP MAKING SENSE

Stop making sense, stop making sense, stop making sense,
making sense.

—David Byrne

I don't have to tell *you* how fun it is *not* to make sense, to take a break and toss your words into a state of mumbo jumbo. There's real benefit to sending sense on a vacation every now and then, especially if you want to shake up your imagination. Sometimes all you need is a gentle nudge (or shove) out of your tidy meaning-making routine. You know, a friendly jab of encouragement to engage in some reckless sentence "mistakes," to string a few dozen words together that fall down laughing, not caring if they're ever read, heard, or seen. Do a handstand or a series of cartwheels before you start. Slow dance through the house with the cat. Serenade the dog. Rescue a spider and release it onto a leaf. Pull a short story off the shelf, begin reading from the last period, and advance *left,* back to the beginning.

Not making sense (or imagining strange things that could never happen, like waking up as a bug or time traveling by holding a baseball card) can be harder for some of us than others. We can be well trained and too often tip the scales toward the rational. To write something that's nonsense, though grammatically correct, can take practice. Don't shy away. If you fall back into sense-making mode, pick yourself up, dust yourself off, and start again. Say what you don't want to do right now. Write it down. (Yes, even write "I don't want to write nonsense, Karen.") Then start at the last word, and write it as your first word. Keep reversing the *entire* order until you have a few nonsense sentences.

Finish the phrase: "Here's what I don't want to do right now . . ." Then start reversing the words until you've reversed the entire order. For example: "library the to books overdue my return or sandwich zucchini a eat, bath a cat skunky the give, or again trash the out take to refuse I . . . deliver to have I speech the finish or dishwasher the unload to want don't I."

Drop Deeper

- Put verbs in places where nouns usually go, and vice versa. Don't fret if you slip back into meaning—it's bound to happen. Bottom line: have fun.

- She tooth-stepped over her under and wasped into flight. So what if heaven and pickles aren't many she paraded to peer upon her refusing. And listing the disk, the dark, the breath. Oh, the sweet tether of fault lines and attention. Not now but more heavy than never this tour of last winter's tomorrow.

- Write one *looong*, ranty sentence, using as many commas, dashes, semicolons as needed. Or a poem of nonsense verse like Lewis Carroll's "Jabberwocky," the first stanza of which was written for the enjoyment of his family. Find the whole poem, which was originally featured as part of his novel

Through the Looking-Glass and What Alice Found There. Even Carroll claimed that he didn't know what some of the words meant!

'Twas brillig, and the slithy toves
Did gyre and gimble in the wabe;
All mimsy were the borogoves,
And the mome raths outgrabe.

Your Turn

LAST
THANKSGIVING

No one remembered to shop for the bird, as Dad calls it, so we end up at Billie's Diner across the street from the Greyhound Bus Station. I'm standing at the door next to my sister, cold air biting through my tights as I read the holiday menu scribbled on a whiteboard above the cash register. At the counter, three men hunch over their dinners. My chin is a quivering knot. I have to focus to keep the flood of tears in my head dammed up.

"Come on, let's try." Mom links her arm through mine and shoots my father a look that says, *This better be good*. My sister says, "Yuck-y." Dad tells us to go sit down.

The waitress places a chipped tureen of something steamy-green in the middle of the table. She looks at me and smiles. "Happy Turkey Day."

"This looks delicious." My mother is wearing her usual enthusiasm.

I don't want to celebrate like this. I want to be home, setting the table while my sister folds the white cloth napkins that I'll refold, when she goes back to the kitchen for the silverware.

"I mean it," I say. "I'm not eating this crap." I want a reaction from my father.

My father ignores me. My sister scoots closer. Mom locks her brown eyes on mine and shoots her *Straighten up* look. She reaches for the ladle and stirs the thick green soup.

I tear the napkin in my lap in half and fix my gaze on the wall. I know my mother doesn't like eating Thanksgiving dinner in a run-down diner, but she won't admit it. Instead she'll call it an "adventure." *Adventure* is her word for an event too terrible to call a disaster.

Dad just eats his soup and stares out the smudged window, watching the silver buses leave the lot across the street. My sister asks a knock-knock joke. I roll my eyes and slide out of the booth to use the ladies' room. My sister gets up, too. She'll follow me anywhere.

The cramped, windowless room smells of urine and old perfume. I warn her not to touch the toilet seat and explain how the diner is filled with germs. While she pees, I stand at the mirror to examine a pimple on the side of my nose.

"I hate him."

"Don't be mad, Kare."

"Don't touch anything," I warn again. "Here." I hold the faucet on with a fist of toilet paper while she pumps gooey pink soap from the dispenser.

She looks into the mirror at me with pleading eyes, but I turn away.

"Come on," I demand. "It'll serve him right if we all get sick."

"Why?"

"Because," I say, as if that is a good enough answer.

Slice of Your Life

- Put "Why" at the top of your page and write as many questions (and questions within questions) within this framework as you can. When you finish one question, leap to another (why did you . . . why do I . . . why can't we . . . why is there . . . why does the . . . why won't you . . .). When you can't write anymore, put "Why not" at the top of your page, and start again.

- Write about a holiday tradition, or a holiday that strayed from tradition.
- Who did you share the last holiday with? Where? What did you eat? What's something you remember saying? What's something someone else said?
- Make anyone who reads your description hungry or thirsty for what you're writing about. Or make them feel disgusted, and not want to take another look (steamy-green soup in a chipped tureen), much less take a bite.

Your Turn

WOULD YOU RATHER . . .

Make the decision, make it with confidence, and the world will be yours.

—Jaren L. Davis

found a card deck at a garage sale last Saturday, sitting on a table between a soup ladle and a plastic bag of checkers. The deck was red with black lettering. The only thing printed on the front was WOULD YOU RATHER? Intrigued, I picked it up, read the first ten cards, and began wondering *which* option I'd choose. I told myself I *had* to choose. Sometimes I play this way, to see which direction my mind moves.

Up the ante on yourself, and conjure up five or ten choices of what *you'd* rather do. You know: "I would rather eat a sawdust sandwich than a bowl of steamy-green soup with hair. I would rather have a third eye than a horn on my head," and so on. Answer as many of the questions on the next page as you can stomach, and then go ask a friend. (You can add details to each question to make it tougher to answer.) Combine some into an "I Would Rather" repetition poem, arranging, layering, detailing your most bizarre choices.

Would You Rather . . .

Tell someone you love them or kiss a frog?
Dance in your underwear in class or always have wet hair?
Have no friends or no computer?
Have your eyes glued shut or your lips glued shut?
Have a six-foot tongue or three ears?
Be three feet tall or eight feet tall?
Have glow-in-the-dark hair or glow-in-the-dark skin?
Do a hundred push-ups or a hundred sit-ups?
Have your grandfather's name or your pet's name?
Eat rotten eggs or drink sour milk?
Eat a hair sandwich or an earwax omelet?
Be stung by a bee or scratched by a cat?
Have golf clubs for legs or tennis rackets for arms?
Take an ice-cold shower or a bath in dirty water?
Lick a dirty foot or drink toilet water?
Swim with sharks or wrestle an alligator?
Smell like rotten eggs or smell like onions?
Sit on a cactus or kiss a frog?
Be a rock or a tree?
Skip recess or skip your birthday for a year?
Have an extra toe or an extra finger?
Eat thirty pounds of cheese or a gallon of peanut butter?
Be the most popular kid or the smartest kid in school?
Be surprised or told in advance?
Eat dinner for breakfast, or breakfast for dinner?
Be hurled through a hurricane or ripped to sea by a tidal wave?
Change the past or clearly see your future?
Answer in extreme detail or one-liners forever?

LAY IT ALL ON THE PAGE AND SWAY

Love the trees until their leaves fall off, then encourage them
to try again next year.

—Chad Sugg

Lay on your back on the carpet, or on a bed of leaves. Relax the bones of your face. Unknit your brow. Let your eyes rest heavy in their sockets. Unclench your jaw. Release your tongue to be the slug that it is. Play rubber lips and feel your gums. Roll your head side to side. Take the deepest inhale and exhale of your life, forgetting all about whirling words for a while.

When ready, imagine the roof above you blown off and the endless depth of sky. Hug your knees to your chest, roll forward and back, making a swing of your spine. With momentum, propel yourself *up, up, up* to standing. Fan out your toes, press weight into the four corners of your feet, and send down thick roots, three times your height, into the center of the earth. Balancing on one foot, bring the other foot to rest on your calf. Then grow the branches of your arms into the air. Challenging yourself, close your eyes and sway in the breeze.

In yoga, this is called the tree pose. (If you fall, congratulate yourself. This means you're taking a risk.) Rebalance on the opposite foot and imagine your favorite tree—redwood, pine, spruce, willow. When ready, bring this same strong-rooted stance into your writing practice.

Pick up your pen, and set your treelike impressions on the page. Is there a rush of gravity up your legs? What are some things that cause your life to sway? If a feeling of tenderness or loss (or snorts of laughter) creep up, add that to what you write about. It's OK if your writing wobbles. It's OK to write without knowing where you'll end up. It's OK *not* to end up.

Drop Deeper

- Write *without* a destination and find out: who's the one you miss the most . . . who's the one who's always there . . . who's the one with the best dance moves or most focused yoga pose?
- Write half a page and begin with, "I didn't know I loved . . ." In detail discover how many things you didn't know about.
- Become something in nature and offer seven lines of advice.

From *Advice from a Tree*

Stand tall and proud
Sink your roots into the Earth
Be content with your natural beauty

Go out on a limb
Drink plenty of water
Remember your roots
Enjoy the view!

—Alan Shamir

Your Turn

Suddenly a Story.....

THE ANGEL OF INSPIRATION AND TRUE VISION

On the day Lizzy was born, tree limbs snapped and the north wind hollered its lonely howl. Twelve tigers of inspiration pounced and bounded into her heart as she twisted her way into the early morning light. White roses opened. Clouds huddled close. She was not afraid to cry and laugh at the same time. She had no idea that her imagination would expand out to touch the silky edge of the sky, where joy meets sorrow and yesterday means nothing to tomorrow. Who knew she'd like the scent of crushed lavender and lemons? Who knew she'd collect heart-shaped stones or find a stray dog in the hollow of a log, give him a name, and lead him home? On the day she was born, the wind's generosity rattled the upstairs windows. Peace brought over apple turnovers and a basket of ripe pears. Excitement somersaulted across the lawn, to catch her newborn attention. On the day she was born, this girl Lizzy, who reminds me of me, was not afraid to dance with the Angel of True Vision, who took her by the hand, led her deeper into the whispered world, and has never let her go.

Story Starters

- Finish these lines:

  On the day I was born, I was not afraid to _____.
  (You can write your story or write in a persona [see page 28] to hang a story from.)

  Little waves of _____ (how did they move?)

  Who knew my imagination could _____

  Who knew one day I'd travel to _____

  Who knew I'd like the scent of _____

  Who knew I would love collecting _____

  Who knew I would one day find _____

- Pick an angel: Short Story Angel, Rooftop Angel, Angel of Long Voyages, Angel of Flames, Snow Angel, Thunder Angel, Rainbow Angel, Angel of Mountain Bike Rides, Angel of Three-Point Shots, and so on. Somewhere have an angel take *you* by the hand and lead you deeper into your journey. Optional: Add this to what you wrote above.

Your Turn

A ROUNDUP OF WORDS

I like the construction of sentences and the juxtaposition
of words—not just how they sound or what they mean,
but even what they look like.

—Don DeLillo

Round up a few words to trot out after "of," then use these words to build out the second half of the juxtaposition image-fragments on the next page. Juxtaposition is another way to make a metaphor. Simply by setting two or more unlike words together and using the connecting word *of*—presto—your ears (and your reader's ears) can't help but pay attention in a whole new way. *But what words do I use?* you ask. Find your magic word bag (see page 159) or use a day of the week, a month, a subject in school, a type of weather, the name of a flower, a tree, a street, a song title, a feeling; any animal, vegetable, mineral, or handy noun: *skydivers, time, history, poetry, midnight, rock and roll, prowling cats, slithering snakes, nibbling mice.* The possibilities are practically endless. Then mess around with syntax (word order) and watch your metaphors morph into poems.

Do *whatever* it takes to make your lines spark and catch metaphorical fire. Play off, mix, blend, tie together, connect words you like the sound, feel, look, taste of. Whatever you do, though, resist the spell of the "correct," "right," or "polite" way of answering. No flock of birds, no gallery of pictures, no stadium of shouting fans allowed at this round-up.

- The tangle of time turns into a slow dance of poetry. The swarm of nervous laughter during first period turns into the rush and tumble of a rock-and-roll earthquake of bright-eyed poets rolling through sixth grade.

A swarm of
The whisper of
A quick roundup of
The stark wilderness of
A tangle of
A gallery of
A heartbreaking story of
The magic of
A flock of
A surprise party of
Snapshots of
Fifteen minutes of
A light laser of
An ocean of
Snatches of
A snowstorm of
An earthquake of

Some yawning chasm of
A sandstorm of
A chunk of
Small acts of
Topped with a dollop of
A rush and tumble of
A free throw of
Accumulated bones of
The first full day of
A stadium of
The in and out of
A quick circle of
My backyard of
The lost music of
From every corner of
A flight of
Through the eyes of

Two minutes of
A bottle of
The long-ago summer of
A hard-hitting tale of
From the heart of
A royal wedding of
A slam dunk of
One rule of
The other end of
A zigzag of
Shout-outs of
Unlined pages of
A hangout of
A three-day weekend of
A small song of
The lost city of
The tumble of

ELEGY

An elegy is a song or single poem of mourning, expressing a loss or grief *without*—and here's the hard part—slipping into self-pity or sentimentality. Typically written for a person who has died, an elegy expresses the author's feelings. I wrote an entire book of poems on the grief of nearly losing my sister, when no amount of sunshine, chocolate, long hikes, or class IV rafting trips with my river guide boyfriend could heal the brokenhearted place inside of me.

Sometimes it's only *through* the process of writing—poems, journal entries, stories, songs, broken bits of our thoughts and feelings—that we find a way to transform our sadness and grief into art. Sandy Diamond, a poet and calligrapher friend, created a sign for me that hangs near my bookshelf. *Artists are healed by their art*, it reads, and in my case, this was true. Sometimes our *biggest* hurts and losses can *only* fit into the *smallest* of spaces, like an elegy. It's then, however, that you start to own your sadness and grief instead of *it* owning you.

Originally, elegies in Greek and Roman literature were poems composed in couplets, or two-line stanzas. (One category, the pastoral elegy, has its roots in Greek and Sicilian poetry of the third and second centuries B.C.) There's no set length anymore for an elegy, and though the *tone*—the way the poem *sounds*—

is generally melancholy, you can of course find another way to express your grief. We all grieve in our own way and in our own time. There's no standard method, manual, or time frame. (See What They Tell You to Forget on page 233.)

Walt Whitman wrote an elegy on the death of Abraham Lincoln called "When Lilacs Last in the Dooryard Bloom'd." A contemporary poet named Catherine Barnett, one of my absolute favorites, wrote an entire book of elegies called *Into Perfect Spheres Such Holes Are Pierced* about the death of her two young nieces in a plane crash. It's a collection that reads like a novel, and one to study on how to hold the reins of self-pity while writing about grief.

C minus A and B equals—
Tree with no branch equals—

What grief looks like:
A knife rusted in the side of a goat.

No, no.
A coin falling in water

And the fish dart for it.

—Catherine Barnett

RENTED ROOMS

We hold hands and walk the sidewalk along Second Street in downtown San Jose, to our father's apartment. My sister says my name in the way that makes me answer *It'll be OK, Al,* even when I'm not sure it will be. We climb through dusty slices of sunlight to apartment 302 to sort through his belongings on the third floor, where the curtains are stained and the carpet's worn thin. I think about how, after our father left Red Bluff that last winter, the birds got disoriented. One flew into the upstairs window—stunned, it lay on the sidewalk by the juniper bush, its feathers splayed in a way that made me want to hold its brokenness in my hands forever, until my mother warned how birds in the wild carry disease, so I left it where it landed and walked back upstairs. Each day, I watched it decompose a little more, until finally a breeze lifted what was left and carried part of me away. Stray images of Red Bluff follow me. I think of that night spying on my parents, how my father walked past me, not knowing I was there, and went to pack his clothes into cardboard. He got into his pickup and drove to stay with friends, go fishing, forget. We talked to him a few times that first year, at Christmas, our birthdays. I remember my mother signing papers and talking to a lawyer. I remember not wearing a coat so I could feel the cold wind in my bones. At school, I acted brave by smiling and making sure I got good grades.

Now my sister and I are taking mouse-steps into a kitchen that smells of garbage and dirty dishwater. The countertop is cluttered and sticky. On the floor next to the stove I spot the wok our father used to pack on camping trips. It's the wok he'd run a finger across, when I forgot to dry it and hang it on the hook above the stove. A layer of grease and caked-on scrambled eggs stick to the bottom. On the front of the refrigerator a coupon for baked beans is taped. A carton of rocky road ice cream sits in the frosted-over freezer. It's the sight of that butcher block, though, that makes me love the man who spent hours kneading down bread dough he'd cover with a dish towel. Our father listened to jazz, brewed sun tea on the deck, reminded us to wipe the rim of the honey jar before tightening the lid back on. Staring at the waving cobwebs, the stale smell of cigarettes hanging in the air between us, I push open a window and tell my sister to forget about the man who died here. I want to remember the man who attached solar panels to the roof, built us a jungle gym, clapped at our dance recitals. Our father was the man who insisted we put away our crayons and wash our hands before we ate the dinner he made. We leave everything the way we find it in that hollowed-out apartment on the third floor. Nothing else except that wok and our memories belong with us.

Slice of Your Life

- Finish this sentence: I could tell the second I stepped through the doorway I wasn't staying . . .
- What event most changed your life? Begin your memoir with a one- or two-word sentence.
- Where does your or someone else's secret sneaking-off lead? If you aren't sure, make it up until you are.
- Describe the contents of a kitchen.

Your Turn

REVISION

Good writing *rarely* comes out whole. OK, sometimes it does, but more often good writing requires rewriting, editing, sculpting, shaping, deleting, and erasing. Revision can be fun, especially when you know someone who can ask the right questions and offer suggestions about what to keep and what to cut away in a clear-sighted way.

At least one or more of the following revision techniques will work every time. Guaranteed. You just have to find the right suggestion to fit your particular poem or story, essay or memoir. I forget where exactly all these useful tips arrived from, but I've studied revision with some of the best. Among them: Jane Hirshfield, Kim Addonizio, Sharon Olds, Molly Fisk, Steve Kowit, Natalie Goldberg, David St. John, Gary Thompson, and Terry Ehret. A pure teaching is sweet and gives us permission to share that sweetness with others. Feel free to pass along to anyone in need of revision tips what you find useful from this chapter. And if you can take a workshop with one of the teachers listed above, do. You *won't* be sorry.

- What's the part in your piece with magic? Underline it. Use it to start a *new* poem or story.
- Which word, line, sentence sings *off* the page? Memorize it. Take it for a walk. Rewrite it in your head. Return to your desk and scribble down what you remember. Keep this; ditch the rest.

- Close your eyes and point blindly to the middle of your piece, then open your eyes and add details to the end of the nearest line: new verbs, strong adjectives, proper nouns, sounds, flavors, colors.
- Ask yourself: *Is there more to be said? Is there more that wants to be said?* Jane Hirshfield taught me this. To which I'll add, "OK, now say it."
- Rewrite your poem backward, word by word, sentence by sentence, or line by line. My friend Terry Ehret calls this a reversal. Though it doesn't work for every poem, it has changed the life of a few of mine.
- Change the pronouns in your writing—change "I" to "she" or "he." Or change "I" to "you." Or the other way around. Mix it up. Take a break from the ego-filled "I," unless of course you're writing using a persona.
- Perform some surgery. Cut off the beginning and/or the end of your poem or story. Stitch lines from another one of your poems into the one you're operating on. Remove three to five lines to see if you really need them. Sometimes the lines we're *most* in love with are the ones that have to go. Sorry! A college English professor, Lennis Dunlap, a proper southern gentleman who called me "Ms. Benke," referred to this as "drowning your pretty little kittens."
- Eliminate *all* adjectives, then put only three back in. Eliminate *all* adverbs (words that end in "ly") and *don't put any back in.* Take out *all* the weak verbs (is, was, has, does, goes), give them verb vitamins, and send them charging back in. Strong verb examples: *wheel, sweep, curl, cut, pack, flex, thread, sew,* and of course, *leap.*
- Force yourself to cut exclamation marks. They are kind of like laughing at your own joke.
- Ask someone close to you to read and revise your piece as if it was *their own.* Keep the parts of the revision you like. Whoever you ask is sure to be flattered.

- Put your poem, story, creative fragment away for a week, a month, a year, or longer. The next time you pull it out, read it as though you are *not* the writer, and make changes. The changes will probably come fast and feel easy. You'll wonder why you didn't see the problems before. (You were too close.) Time's the *best* editor.
- Change the way the entire thing sits on the page. Flip it around. Shake it up. Toss it around. Be bold. Keep only the words that fall back down and stick.
- Amy Hempel suggests, "Sometimes a flat-footed sentence is what serves, so you don't get all writerly: 'He opened the door.' There, it's open."

Tip

Take a paragraph or a few stanzas from one of your poems and apply at least two of the above suggestions. Have—or pretend to be having—fun as you do this. Remember: revision, too, can be oh-so creative.

QUESTIONS ONLY YOU CAN ANSWER

I am not young enough to know everything.

—*Oscar Wilde*

Sometimes we can get in the habit of thinking the right answer is *out there*, waiting in a book somewhere, or in the head of someone who has more experience and expertise, when really our most important answers already live inside our hearts and have been with us since we were born. We just haven't quieted down long enough to hear their wisdom.

For the questions below, whatever drifts into your mind is fine. If you can imagine it and catch it, you can write it. You can always go back later and add more details and nouns, swap out verbs, erase adverbs, take out a few adjectives. You're the president, the king, the queen, the CEO, the top dog of your writing, so put on your crown or jeweled collar. You're *filled* with your own unique light that *never* stops shining, though at times you might feel it grows dim. These are questions to which only *you* know the answer. So go ahead, search inside—be brave. Write them.

From where does your darkness come? Your light?

- My darkness comes from an interrupting sound, the clearing of
- the critic's throat, complete with two permanent scowl lines be-
- tween her eyes. My light arrives in the form of an equation, com-
- bining every poem I'll ever know with the ease of a long embrace,
- a smile set loose across my soul.

What crushes your truth? _____

What might a hundred questions overflow into? _____

How did luck get so lucky? _____

What happens to your world when the sun's rays tremble?

_____

What do you see when you walk through yellow light? (Keep answering, walking through all the colors of a rainbow.)

_____

Where do you drift when the water is deep? _____

_____

OXYMORONS

Be realistic: plan for a miracle.

—*Osho*

An *oxymoron* is a figure of speech that combines contradictory terms. The most common oxymorons involve an adjective-noun combo. They can be a pair of words, or they can be created by sentences or phrases. Here are some oxymoron quotes and some one, two, three (or more) word oxymorons that I've read, heard, and overheard. Add some of your favorites to this list, or select ones to pull out and use in an oxymoron poem that reads like a novel.

"Drive slowly, we're in a hurry."—Winston Churchill to his chauffeur

"I never said most of the things I said."—Yogi Berra

"Life can only be understood backward; but it must be lived forward."—Soren Kierkegaard

"Tell them to stand closer apart."—Samuel Goldwyn

They say it's not as bad as they say it is.

On one hand, I'm indecisive; but on the other, I'm not.

Everything is so random, there must be a pattern.

Two wrongs don't make a right, but three rights make a left.

Walking up stairs gets me down.

You always find something in the last place you look.

Doublespeak	Organized mess
Bittersweet	Forgotten memory
Jumbo shrimp	Friendly takeover
Same difference	Alone in a crowd
Old news	The sound of silence
Virtual reality	An open secret
Controlled chaos	The living dead

10,000 NAMES FOR RAIN

Prartho (P-*Roar*-Toe) returns from India with a red bindi on her forehead, though inside she's feeling blue, thinking about her teacher a continent away whom she misses more than she can say. Outside the laundromat on Miller Avenue she sits in her car, waiting for her sheets and pillowcases to dry. Only after a while, she begins to hear her teacher's voice encouraging her to play a game with the rain of her sadness. The February evening is misty. She still has to stop at the market to shop for dinner, her daughters up the road, waiting for her. She longs for all that she cannot yet name, so gazes into the sky and starts to make up "10,000 Names for Rain." Through foggy windows she calls out: *Soft and Steady on the Steel Blue Roof.* Then *The Mourners Who Left for the Mountains . . . The Song of Missing Him . . . The Bringing Down of Summer Leaves . . . The Smell of Pine Trees . . . The Memory of Mr. Porreca Fishing in His Raincoat.* She calls the rain *The Whoosh of Walking through Sand.* She names it *What the Sun Will Never Know.* It's this easy for Prartho, who slips out of feeling lost and wraps a shawl of possibility around her slender shoulders. Soon, heading up the highway, she holds a new poem, and begins to sing about being just an ordinary woman, with a pile of clean clothes in the backseat and the power to rename whatever life—and her teacher—sends her way.

Story Starters

- Describe where you are, and then choose something to re-name (the night, the moonlight, love, snow, a lost hour, the cat, a country, your missing of someone near or far) and play the game that Prartho made up.
- Take a bath and rename *yourself* while you float. Make sure to use plenty of soap for bubbles and as many dashes as you need.

Midnight-Soaker-Sulker.   Bendy-Body-Poet-Whose-Hamstrings-Howl.   Lover-of-the-Full-Moon-and-Ripe-Kumquats.   Dreamer-of-Wild-Horses-Who-She-Will-Ride-Again.   Once-Upon-a-Time-Soccer-Warrior-No-More.   Collector-of-Stillness-and-Star-Shine. Shy-Sorcerer-Who-Skips-Shimmies-and-loves-the-Hula.

Your Turn

SCATTERING HIS ASHES

We drive down the Pacific Coast Highway eating Fig Newtons and listening to a CD my sister made with the songs we like from The Smiths, Modern English, Dave Matthews Band. We sip from water bottles and talk about words we fear, picking them out of the air.

"*Swerves*," I say, and grip the steering wheel.

"*Alligators*," she pokes my arm.

She unwraps a pack of gum and we compete for the biggest bubble. We sing to our favorite songs. *There's nothing the two of us can't do. I dream of a world, the kind which never hates. I'll stop the world and melt with you.* We don't exclude anything. Not the world's fragile beauty. Not the watery field rolling out to meet the horizon. Not my fear of snakes or her fear of shadows. I tell her how *cats* and *poetry* keep me from getting lost. She tells me the sound of *rain* reminds her of the random way our hearts beat in tandem.

"Life moves in all directions," I explain.

"Like Dad." She reaches for my hand.

We pull into the state park at Big Sur a little after 3 P.M. I let the ranger know we'll only be staying a couple of hours. My sister asks if he'll waive the fee. *It's so late in the day*, she smiles and offers him a piece of gum. He attaches a sticker to our windshield and waves us through. We know where we're going. We park at the trailhead of the gorge. We used to hike here with our parents, in the seventies, when Mom skinny-dipped and Dad dove from the highest cliff. Hiking back now, we each step over the word *suicide,* the same way we skirt around a fallen tree. At water's edge, we sit. Our fingers meet inside a plastic bag. I release the first handful to the wind. She examines the splintered shards—some the size of fingernails, some larger. That winter before our father left, he'd stood on a bridge above the Sacramento River, stretched his arms into the wind, and pretended to fly. We'd walked out to see how high the river had risen during the storm. Looking back at us, he'd said, "It's not the length of a lifetime that matters, but what does or doesn't fit inside." At the time, I didn't understand and had probably rolled my eyes and muttered, "Whatever."

We take turns now rinsing our hands of grief and shame, and as my sister slips a piece of ash into her pocket, I want to ask if she thinks she can keep a part of him with her. Instead I tell her we were both his favorite and watch her eyes soften in the afternoon's yellow glow.

Afterward, we gather up all our words and hike back to the car in silence. We drive the curvy road up the coast, and look for horses grazing Ventana's hills. She points to an Appaloosa and calls it her own. I tell her that she's mine.

Our cousin meets us at our mother's house. It's late when we arrive, so we tiptoe upstairs and change into our pajamas. I examine my sunburn. Dawnie finds a tube of aloe vera. My sister talks about her new boyfriend, wondering when he'll call, when she should say *I love you.* We brush and floss our teeth, try on moisturizers and lip balms, finishing each other's sentences and offering advice. It's the part of being together that makes me want to hold on to all the secrets we've ever swapped, all the stories we've entrusted. I don't want to think about tomorrow, when we'll travel in different directions, back into our separate lives. Tonight, in our mother's house by the water, her dog asleep on the landing outside our door, we Ro-Sham-Bo over who takes the spot in the middle, rearrange the blankets, and swap firm pillows for soft. I hold gratitude for the girls we were, who grew up together, who survived together, who share tears and now laugh together about something in the dark no one has to find words for.

Slice of Your Life

- What words are you scared of? What words keep you safe? Somewhere in your writing include a lyric or two from a song.
- Reflect on a road trip *and* a conversation. Combine the two.
- Name a person who makes you happy. Include one wish for them *and* the world. Turn it into a half-page, real-life story.

Your Turn

EXIT, THIS WAY . . .

One last thing before you go: keep writing. Even if you're midsentence and the bell rings. Even if the teacher says, "Pencils down," but you still have more to say. I mean it. Those ideas coursing through your mind, heart, imagination, down your arm and out your hands and fingers, those bursts and blasts of poetic truth, will *not* return in the same way again. Ever. And you don't want to lose them. Not-a-one. It can be challenging to find your way into the deepest portals of yourself. So once you've mapped a narrow path in and are crossing a stream of similes or climbing a steep hill of a story to whatever image you need to retrieve, *don't stop for anything*. OK, except maybe a fire drill.

To write well, you know now that you *must* first pay attention to your life and take an interest in what's happening inside of you, no matter how loud the voices outside you get. In our current century of cell phones, iChat, Twitter, Facebook, instant messaging, texting, and fast, faster, fastest achievement-oriented modes of being—which I get is *soooo* enticing—this slowing down and finding a calm field in which to sit and pick up a pen to unwind your life grows more important. Writing is about telling your truths—and truth, in my experience, doesn't react well when distracted, rushed, imposed upon, or told to *hurry up*. So slow down. Poetic truth has its own rhythm, and requires a lot of space and downtime, *without* deadlines. Poetic truth wants to get close to that part of *you* that needs to dream BIG in order for your emerging voice, characters, and narrator to step into his or her own light and really shine.

So make a pact, just for today, to trust yourself. Pick up a pen and send your critic away from where you write. Stay in your pajamas with your notebook and a stack of cinnamon toast.

Invite your muse over who's *always* rooting for you to get silly, be foolish, let the characters in your stories dig holes to China in the backyard or climb Mt. Everest, if that's what they want to do. Your poems and stories want to *find you*. Your muse will offer up all manner of surprising situations for this to happen, if you carve out the space to hang out with him or her. Go way *in there*, feel your fear and tunnel in deeper. Your writing path will take you to the exact territory on the page where you need to be. Then look around, learn the land, the river, who you're traveling with. I'm thinking about you right now on this grand adventure, as you leap write in and begin another page.

ACKNOWLEDGMENTS

Thank you to my agent, Stefanie Von Borstel, for taking a risk that day in Austin, Texas; the creative team at Shambhala/Roost Books, especially Jennifer Urban-Brown, who for a second time has guided another of my book-children into the world; Jennifer Campaniolo, for assistance on the publicity path; Julia Gaviria, for oh-so-helpful copyediting suggestions; Lora Zorian, for her design flair; and Joy Gosney, for the artistry and lettering that make my book covers leap off the shelf.

A deep bow to Ed Sattizahn and Vimala Sangha, namaste to Maritza, Christy Brown, and James Higgins for guidance on and off the mat, and gratitude to Dr. Piers Barry, Chris Darden, Jan Edl Stein, and Richard Lipfield for their healing help.

Kudos to California Poets in the Schools and to Terri Glass for her long-time commitment; to Wyeth Stiles, Travis Woods, and Mark Grothman for high-tech assistance for a low-tech girl. Appreciation to Jane Hirshfield, kindhearted teacher and friend; to Prartho Sereno, a constant source of playful wisdom and inspiration; and to Kathy Evans, Linda Wolfe, Susan Wooldridge, Dana Lomax, Sasha Eckle-Sanchez, Claire Blotter, giovanni singleton, Lea Aschkenas, Michele Rivers, Karen Lewis, Susan Sibbit, Judyth Collin, Molly Fisk, Ruth Gendler, Natalie Goldberg, and the long list of poet-teachers from whom I learn my craft. Hugs to the young and young-at-heart student-poets I have the privilege of meeting on and off the page, especially Zoe McCormack and the Experimental Tween Writer-Snackers (you know who you are) for your trust and willingness. And to

Yolanda Fletcher, senior children's librarian at the Mill Valley Public Library, for her insightful book recommendations.

Love and more love to my family and friends for their support and generosity of heart, especially Owen, Collin, and Clive Prell; Alison and Brad Altmann; Dawn, Matt, and Luc Antonelli; Brian Lewis, Joan Kip, Lynn Mundell, Barbara Rounds, Michelle, Andy, and Max Lester, Albert Flynn DeSilver, Sean Perry, Carol Anderson, Mary Lea Crawley, Kristin Laymon, Amy and Jesse Pearson, Sasha Faulkner, Jack Creston, Julie Westcott, Russ Mitchell, Christopher Miles, Devatara Holman; Courtney, Marco, Nicholas, and Sebi della Cava; Carolyn Ingram, Cathy Carmadelle, Carin Garland, Tammara Norman, and Edwin and Anna Hamilton. Finally, hand to heart to Don and Marlene Benke, and Allen and Nina Nelson, for their boundless encouragement and steadfast belief. Your light surrounds me, your love supports me.

BOOKS AND RESOURCES

Books That Inspired Me While Creating *Leap Write In!*

Beamish Boy by Albert Flynn DeSilver

The Book of Qualities by J. Ruth Gendler

California Poets in the Schools Statewide Anthologies 1992–present

Finding What You Didn't Lose by John Fox

Given Words by Elizabeth White

The House on Mango Street by Sandra Cisneros

How to Be an Explorer of the World by Keri Smith

Imagination Comes to Breakfast by Kathy Evans

Leaping Poetry edited by Robert Bly

Lives of the Heart poems by Jane Hirshfield

Making Your Own Days by Kenneth Koch

Micro Fiction by Jerome Stern

Of This World by Joseph Stroud

Phone Call from Paris, Everyday Miracles: An A to Z Guide to the Simple Wonders of Life, and *Causing a Stir: The Secret Lives & Loves of Kitchen Utensils* by Prartho Sereno

poemcrazy by Susan Goldsmith Wooldridge

The Poet's Companion by Kim Addonizio and Dorianne Laux

Quote Poet Unquote edited by Dennis O'Driscoll

Sister by Karen Benke

Stories of the Poets by Suzi Mee

Taming Your Gremlin by Richard D. Carson

The Triggering Town by Richard Hugo

Wabi-Sabi for Artists, Designers, Poets & Philosophers by Leonard Koren

Walking on Alligators by Susan Shaughnessy

Wherever You Go, There You Are by Jon Kabat-Zinn

Wild Mind and *Writing Down the Bones* by Natalie Goldberg

The Writer's Block by Jason Rekulak

Writing without Teachers by Peter Elbow

Resources

100 WORD STORY

www.100wordstory.org

This online literary publication is fun. Editors Grant and Lynn offer a monthly theme and a monthly photo prompt. You can write prose poems or flash fiction. The only requirement is that your submission be exactly 100 words.

826 NATIONAL

www.826national.org

826 centers offer students ages six to eighteen free opportunities to explore their creativity, improve their writing skills, and strengthen their own voices. Centers are located in Ann Arbor, Boston, Chicago, Detroit, Los Angeles, New York City, San Francisco, Seattle, and Washington, D.C. (826 Valencia in San Francisco has a pirate supply store with temporary tattoos, belly-of-a-whale escape kits, and mermaid bait.)

CALIFORNIA POETS IN THE SCHOOLS

www.cpits.org

One of the largest writers-in-the-schools programs in the nation, serving students K–12 in more than thirty counties. CPITS proudly taught their one-millionth student poet in 2011! I've taught with CPITS since 1994.

MINDFUL SCHOOLS

www.mindfulschools.org

If you'd like to learn how mindfulness techniques can help you and your writing, reduce stress, help with test anxiety, create a calm place of patience inside you, and strengthen your relationships, then this is the site for you. And if you have a teacher who's a yeller—we've all had a few—slip this Web site onto his or her desk.

NANOWRIMO

National Novel Writing Month

www.nanowrimo.org

Visit this site if you want to write a fifty-thousand-word novel from scratch between 12 A.M. November 1 and 11:59 P.M. November 30. It's not a contest. NaNoWriMo also has a Young Writers Program for participants age seventeen and under.

POET'S HOUSE

www.poetshouse.org

A national poetry library and meeting place in New York City that invites poets and the public to step into the living tradition of poetry.

RECESSITATE

www.orandaworks.com

Instant tools to refresh your class.

TEACHERS AND WRITERS COLLABORATIVE (T&W)

www.twc.org

T&W seeks to educate the imagination by offering innovative creative writing programs for students. T&W also publishes an award-winning quarterly magazine on teaching.

INDEX OF WRITING EXPERIMENTS

A Note to Teachers

For printable samples of activities in *Rip the Page!* and *Leap Write In!*, download a PDF of Karen's surefire ways to get kids and teens excited to pick up a pen and play on the page. Go to www.roostbooks.com/KarenBenkeResources.

ABOUT THE AUTHOR

Credit: Barbara Bowman

Karen Benke is the author of *Sister* (Marina del Rey, Calif.: Conflux Press, 2004) and *Rip the Page!: Adventures in Creative Writing* (Boston: Shambhala, 2010). A creative writing coach and poet-teacher with California Poets in the Schools, she uses playful prompts to guide writers of all ages to greater access of their heart-wisdom and imagination. A recipient of grants and residences from Poets & Writers, Marin Arts Council Fund for Artists, Hedgebrook, and the Djerassi Foundation, she lives north of the Golden Gate Bridge with her family and a cat named Clive. Visit her at www.karenbenke.com for information about bringing her word-ticket "play-shops" to your school, library, book fair, or community event.